PRAISE FOR **CHURCH+HOME**

I honestly believe that discipling my kids is far more important than pastoring National Community Church. NCC can find another pastor. But my kids can't find another dad. Nothing is more important or more challenging than discipling my kids. And I need all the help I can get. I'm so grateful for the Faith@Home focus! I think it helps reorder our priorities: God first, family second, church third.

Mark Batterson
Pastor and author, National Community Church, Washington, D.C.

As a pastor, Mark Holmen demonstrated how a local church could inspire and equip families to instill strong faith in the next generation. As a partner in the Strong Families Innovation Alliance, he has also been a mentor to other leaders who are trying to turn the tide of declining generational faith transference.

Kurt Bruner
Pastor, Spiritual Formation, LakePoint Church, Rockwell, Texas
Executive Director, StrongFamilies Innovative Alliance

As a champion for the Faith@Home movement, Mark Holmen captures the essence of how God is leading churches to push faith back home as the primary place of spiritual influence.

Brian Haynes
Associate Pastor, Kingsland Baptist Church, Katy, Texas
Creator of Legacy Milestones
Author of *Shift: What It Takes to Finally Reach Families Today*

After I read *Building Faith at Home*, it changed my life and my ministry. Modeling the faith at home message is something I missed for a long time on a personal and professional level. This book is a must read for anyone in ministry or anyone with kids. *Church+Home* is practical, biblical and doable. Mark convincingly challenges each of us to start, live and launch our faith at home. I highly recommend this book.

Craig Jutila
Founder, Empowering Kids, Inc. and Orphan Impact International
Author, Speaker and Faith@Home Believer

By including Faith@Home Take It Home events, we are reaching families in a very practical hands-on way and in surprising evangelistic ways.

Melinda Kinsman
Children's Ministry, Elementary, Beaverton Foursquare, Beaverton, Oregon

When our culture went to the service economy, American families outsourced cooking, cleaning, lawn maintenance—and spiritual formation. We decided that the staff and programs at the church could take care of bringing up our children in the faith. What a colossal misassumption! Now Mark Holmen helps us understand how we can resume God conversations where we live—our homes—with the people we live with—our families.

Reggie McNeal
Missional Leadership Specialist, Leadership Network

Take whatever survey result you want; they all show we can do better with our kids ... and we must do better! What Mark has to say speaks right to the partnership between two of the greatest potential sources of influence in our kids' lives—the *Church* and the *family*. For the sake of your kids, please read this book and act on it as God directs.

Jim Mellado
President, Willow Creek Association

Consider Mark's challenge: "Of all the things you can do as a leader in Christ's church, there is nothing more important than helping bring Christ and Christlike living into the center of every home."

Pastor Rob Reinow
Family Pastor and Men's Ministry Pastor, Wheaton Bible Church
Founder, Visionary Parenting (www.VisionaryParenting.com)

MARK HOLMEN

Church+Home

THE PROVEN FORMULA FOR

BUILDING LIFELONG FAITH

Regal

From Gospel Light
Ventura, California, U.S.A.

Published by Regal
From Gospel Light
Ventura, California, U.S.A.
www.regalbooks.com
Printed in the U.S.A.

Originally published as *Building Faith at Home* by Mark Holmen in 2007.
Revised and updated edition published in 2010.

Library of Congress Cataloging-in-Publication Data
Holmen, Mark.
Church + home : the proven formula for building lifelong faith / Mark A. Holmen. —
Rev. and updated ed.
p. cm.
Previous ed. published as: Building faith at home. 2007.
ISBN 978-0-8307-5568-4 (hardcover)
1. Families—Religious life. I. Holmen, Mark. Building faith at home. II. Title.
III. Title: Church and home.
BV4526.3.H645 2010
259'.1—dc22
2010032938

Rights for publishing this book outside the U.S.A. or in non-English languages are
administered by Gospel Light Worldwide, an international not-for-profit ministry.
For additional information, please visit www.glww.org, email info@glww.org, or write
to Gospel Light Worldwide, 1957 Eastman Avenue, Ventura, CA 93003, U.S.A.

1 2 3 4 5 6 7 8 9 10 11 12 13 14 15 16 17 18 / 20 19 18 17 16 15 14 13 12 11 10

To order copies of this book and other Regal products in bulk quantities,
please contact us at 1-800-446-7735.

*I dedicate this book to my father, Arlen, who went
to be with the Lord on November 24, 2004. Dad, you touched
my life in so many ways. You set an example for me in the way
you joyfully served the Lord and followed his call.
You truly lived your life verse from Isaiah 6:8: "Then I heard the
voice of the Lord saying, 'Whom shall I send? And who
will go for us?' And I said, 'Here am I. Send me!' " Thank you for
continuing to cheer me on from your heavenly home,
as I do my best to follow the Lord's leading.
I love you.*

Contents

Foreword

A decade ago, I was a pretty typical church leader, believing that the ministry of the local church should revolve around the needs of its adults. The theory was that if we could effectively reach adults and help them, they would convert that investment into a moral and spiritual windfall for society.

Through a series of God-orchestrated circumstances, in 2001 I began conducting research regarding the development of and ministry to children. From the beginning of that three-year adventure, I considered it "filler"—a kind of bridge between some of the other adult-focused projects in which I was more interested. But God had other ideas. He used that project, which became the basis of the book *Transforming Children into Spiritual Champions*, to wake me up to a critical realization: What you do with children—yours and others—is the most important ministry thrust you will ever undertake.

Why? Because the moral, spiritual and relational foundations of people's lives are determined primarily by the age of 13. After that point, it is very difficult—and rare—to change those moorings. Who a person is by age 13 is pretty much who he or she will be for the rest of his or her life in terms of beliefs, values, morals, relational emphases and ideas about faith. Naturally, the Holy Spirit may intervene at any time and introduce radical transformation, but based on decades of research, I know that such deep-seated change is the exception to the rule.

That eye-opener led to a follow-up research project, which also took several years to complete, in which I studied the parenting practices in homes where the children grow up to become spiritual champions. Once again, the insights, as described in *Revolutionary Parenting*, blew me away as both a parent of young children and as a leader in the church. It became apparent that even in today's culture it is possible to raise spiritual champions, but it does not happen by default; it requires the parents to be strategic and consistent in their child-rearing efforts.

Having now conducted thousands of interviews with parents and children regarding moral and spiritual development, some elements of the process have become crystal clear. For instance, the local church plays a role in the growth of children, but its involvement is not the key to success in raising godly children. The critical factor is what takes place in the home. Parents have an overwhelmingly significant influence on who their children turn out to be. A community of faith can—and should—support parents in that effort, but the responsibility and opportunity to raise God-honoring children are given to the parents.

In short, the moral and spiritual nature of every human being is predominantly shaped by his or her family experience. Parents are responsible for defining their family culture, process and outcomes. In *Church + Home*, you will discover what parents and churches can do together to facilitate parents accepting and mastering the practical realities of raising Christlike young people.

For more than 20 years, our research has consistently shown that success in any transformational endeavor requires that five steps be in place. First, there must be an understanding of the situation in relation to the desired conditions. Second, the leaders of the group in question must be committed to the people and to facilitating the desired outcomes. Third, there must be appropriate strategic thinking and planning that gets converted into focused actions for those outcomes to occur. Fourth, there must be sufficient resources to accomplish the job. Finally, there must be specific and measurable criteria that reflect positive outcomes, such measurement of the criteria must consistently and objectively be performed, and necessary alterations must be made to the process based on those measures.

Mark Holmen discusses these matters in this book, enabling parents and church leaders to convert good intentions into good practices. Using his years of experience as both a family ministry pastor and then as a senior pastor with a special emphasis upon family ministry, he describes the various perspectives and endeavors that are needed to be a church that partners with parents as they prepare children for a life of meaning and purpose through their in-home experiences. Thankfully, this is not a book of theory; it is a volume containing practical, hands-on solutions to the challenges pastors and church leaders face in these trying times, all consistent with biblical principles and tested in the real world.

Whether or not you have young children in your home, *Church + Home* addresses the most important audience your church serves: young people and their families. Use this book as another tool in your toolbox as you seek to restore the heart of our culture, the health of the local church and the vitality of the American family.

George Barna
Ventura, California
April 2007

Acknowledgments

I want to acknowledge the following people who God has used to help shape the Faith@Home vision in me.

To my wife, Maria, who is the true Faith@Home champion in our household. Thank you for being the best partner I could ever have, and for supporting and encouraging me through the process of writing this book and serving this movement.

To my daughter, Malyn, who has taught me so much as your daddy! Thank you for allowing me to talk and write about our experiences together. You are the greatest gift in my life, and I can't thank you enough for the way you pray for me and bless me as your father. You're the best!

To the churches I have had the opportunity to serve: Trinity Lutheran Church in Long Lake, Minnesota; Trinity Lutheran Church in Stillwater, Minnesota; Calvary Lutheran Church in Golden Valley, Minnesota; and Ventura Missionary Church in Ventura, California. Thank you for helping me to grow as a pastor and leader, and for the ways you wholeheartedly supported the Faith@Home vision long before it was a movement. Thanks for being the type of authentic communities that allowed me to follow the Lord's vision and share our experiences along the way. As a result of your faithfulness, God is using you to be a light for other congregations all across the world.

To my mentor, Dr. Dick Hardel, who inspired and motivated me in so many ways. Thanks for your leadership, friendship and encouragement. It's been a lot of fun to see how God has led this movement forward over the years.

To Gospel Light, Focus on the Family Canada and U.S., as well as the Willow Creek Association, and Randall House who have all jumped in to support me and the Faith@Home movement. God has used each of you to help spread the Faith@Home message and vision to church leaders and parents all over the world.

To my mother, Myrne. Thank you for showing me how to love the Lord with all my heart, soul and strength in our home. Thanks for your constant love and support, and for being the best example of Faith@Home living a person could ask for.

Introduction

What Do You Mean When You Say Church + Home?

What Is Church + Home All About?

1. It's about challenging you to look at how you "do" ministry from the perspective of how your ministry is impacting lifestyle behavior at home.
2. It's about making some two-degree changes to how you "do" ministry.
3. It's about providing you with an antidote to hypocrisy.
4. It's about bringing you into a larger movement that God is leading so you can learn from others and become a contributing partner!

Greetings in the name of Christ! My name is Mark Holmen, and I have the privilege of serving as a full-time missionary to the Faith@Home movement (I will explain what this is below) after being a senior pastor at Ventura Missionary Church for 7 years and a youth and family ministry pastor in Minnesota for over 12 years. In 2007, I had the opportunity to write a book to church leaders titled *Building Faith at Home: Why Faith@Home Must Be the Church's #1 Priority*, which inspired and challenged many church leaders across the world to become more Faith@Home focused.

Regal Publishing was preparing to print another quantity of these books, but I suggested that before doing so we should consider revising the book's text because many things have evolved in and through the Faith@Home movement during the past three years. One of the most exciting things that has happened is that many more voices supporting the cause of Faith@Home have emerged, and that is something I have added throughout this book. In addition to this, I have also had the opportunity to travel around the world and see fresh ways that God is working through the Faith@Home movement, and I look forward to sharing these insights and innovations with you as well. So, for some of you, this will be entirely new information, while for others it will be about 50 percent of the same material and 50 percent new content.

So, what is the Faith@Home movement all about? The Faith@ Home movement is about challenging church leaders to look at how we do ministry from the perspective of the impact it is having on lifestyle behavior at home. This is neither a family ministry program nor a movement just for children's ministry leaders; *every ministry* of the church should have an "@Home" focus. Satan has clearly been at work over the last 30 to 50 years to take Christ and Christlike living out of the home. Satan recognizes that what happens in the home is more influential on faith formation than what happens in the church, especially for the next generations of followers, so he has strategically and methodically worked to get 24/7 authentic Christlike living out of the home. Yet, as is always the case, Satan is not going to have the last word. God is responding, through His Church, to reestablish the home as the primary place where faith is nurtured. And just as God used other movements in the past to positively impact and transform the Church, God is doing the same thing through the Faith@Home movement today.

I also feel that it is important to note from the outset that the Faith@Home movement is God's movement, not my movement. Although it will be helpful for you to understand a little bit about who I am and the role I feel God has called me to play in this movement, please do not attach my name as the originator of this movement or give me any credit for it. It is God and God alone who deserves all the glory and praise for it!

Finally, I feel it is important for you to understand a little more about who I am and the role I feel God has called me to play in this movement. As a former senior pastor and children, youth and family ministry pastor, I have had the opportunity to develop and work with the Faith@Home movement in a variety of ministry roles. I have served in small, medium and large churches; and I have been in both denominational and nondenominational settings. Through these experiences God has enabled me to see what has worked and not worked when it comes to challenging and equipping people to be Faith@Home focused. I have also had the privilege of meeting with church leaders in countries like Germany, Norway, Sweden, Canada, Brazil, Switzerland and the Netherlands, and through this I have been able to see how God is working effectively in and through this movement all over the world. Let me share a few exciting things that God has done in just the past three years through the Faith@Home movement.

- In Canada, hundreds of churches have become Faith@Home focused as the Faith@Home movement has spread across the entire country thanks to a series of conferences cosponsored by Focus on the Family and Willow Creek Canada. The Faith@Home movement launched in Canada in 2004, and as a result, we are beginning to see some churches hiring pastors to serve as lead pastors of Faith@Home ministries in that country. To be perfectly honest, Canada is leading the way when it comes to embracing and developing the Faith@Home movement.

- Hundreds of churches in Sweden have become Faith@Home focused. This includes the largest denomination in Sweden, which made the Faith@Home topic the focus of their pastor's conference in 2008.

- In Germany, Norway and the Netherlands, Faith@Home resources have been translated to serve the movement, and the Faith@Home message was the most requested topic for future conferences!

• Brazil, the Pacific Rim, Australia, New Zealand and South Africa will experience the Faith@Home movement in the next few years as it is spread there through the Willow Creek Association's international division.

• In the United States, we are now seeing the Faith@Home movement appear as one of the primary topics at many pastors' conferences. We are also seeing many new books and resources being written on this topic by prominent authors who provide compelling arguments and methodologies for Faith@Home strategies and innovations. Faith@Home is even becoming a topic covered in many seminaries!

I share this with you so you can see that the Faith@Home movement is not a program or fad and that the insights and information you will find in *Church + Home* are not all my own.

Why Church + Home?

This book is not a theological argument against the Church and/or organized religion. I'm not an anti-Church guy; in fact, I'm just the opposite. I love the Church and have served her faithfully for over 20 years. I believe Christ loves the Church as His Bride, and therefore, when we as His followers choose to love and follow Christ, we are also called to love and serve His Church. Yet I do not find any Scripture that supports being one-hour-at-church-only followers of Christ. I do not find any Scripture that supports a drop-off-and-let-the-professionals-do-it mentality that says "it's the Church's job to teach my kids the faith."

I do believe that Scripture is filled with examples and challenges that call us to live out our faith 24/7. I also believe that the Bible is quite clear that parents are the ones who are primarily responsible for passing on the faith to their children (see Deut. 6:4-9; Ps. 78:5-8), not the Church. Therefore the theology of Faith@Home is quite simple: The Church is called to be a lifelong partner (not replacement) with parents to help people *know* God's story, *tell* God's story and *be* God's story 24 hours a day, 7 days a week, beginning in their homes and extending throughout all aspects of their lives.

This simple theology for Faith@Home—and for this book—is based on a simple reality. What happens in the home is more important and influential than what happens at church when it comes to faith formation and behavior. You don't have to be a rocket scientist to realize that we spend way more time at home than we do at church; and at the end of the day, faith is a relationship with Jesus Christ that is to be lived out all the time rather than just for an hour on Sunday mornings. Yet in spite of this obvious reality, the Church has not had a "+ Home" focus. Now, don't get me wrong; it's not that as Church leaders we don't care about what happens at home. We *do* care. But we can and have become consumed with making sure that everything we do at church is the very best it can be. We ask questions such as:

- Are our church programs growing? Did our men's ministry retreat have more men this year than last year?
- Is our facility holding up or in need of change and/or expansion?
- Are we seeing more people being baptized or joining the church?
- Did the sound, lighting and PowerPoint slides all work?
- Did this ministry event (or program) meet budget?
- Did the people respond to the message?

While these are important questions, they are church-centric and don't stretch to include lifestyle behavior at home. A Faith@Home-focused church asks different questions, such as:

- Is our men's ministry equipping our men to be godly singles, husbands, dads and grandpas at home?
- Is our women's ministry equipping our women to be godly singles, wives, moms and grandmas at home?

- Is our singles ministry equipping our singles to live out their faith 24/7 at home and/or college?
- Is our seniors' ministry equipping our grandparents to be meddling Christian grandparents in the lives of their children and grandchildren?
- Is our nursery ministry helping parents recognize that it is their role to serve as the primary influencers of faith formation?
- Is our children's ministry equipping parents to engage in faith talks, devotions, Bible reading, service and worship at home?
- Is our youth ministry equipping our students to live out their faith at home or school, with or even without their parents?
- Does our worship have an @Home focus? What about our mission's ministry?

The questions posed by the Faith@Home-focused church are obviously centered on an outcome different from a program-oriented church.

My prayer is that you will view me as your missionary who, through this book, is bringing you ideas, information and insights about a movement that God is leading and calling you to participate in as well. By the end of this book, I want you to be challenged, inspired and motivated to look at how you can lead in a more Faith@Home-focused manner the ministry you have been called to serve.

CHAPTER SUMMARY

- People are failing to apply faith or biblical living in their everyday life at home.

- We must work to overcome Satan, who clearly and strategically works to get people to not live out their faith at home.

- Religious life in the home is nearly extinct.

- The church "drop-off" approach to teaching faith often doesn't lead to lasting faith.

- Families prosper by impressing faith on their children at home.

- Faith must be caught, not taught, and this is best done in the home.

- Programs geared toward children and youth during the past 40 years haven't instilled a lifestyle of faith.

- Church leaders need to view programs through a new set of lenses that focus on equipping parents to build faith in the home.

- Common problems that churches face include declining youth engagement, parental drop-off mentality, the Church's loss of standing, ill-equipped parents, and competition from the world.

- The challenge is to equip the home to be the primary place for nurturing faith.

What Are We Accomplishing?

The local church should be an intimate and valuable partner in the effort to raise the coming generation of Christ's followers and church leaders, but it is the parents whom God will hold primarily accountable for the spiritual maturation of their children.[1]
GEORGE BARNA

ANOTHER VOICE SAYS...

Rob Rienow, Family Pastor and Men's Ministry Pastor, Wheaton Bible Church
Founder, Visionary Parenting (www.VisionaryParenting.com)

My journey with the Faith@Home reformation began in my own home. After 10 years of full-time youth ministry, God brought me to a place of deep repentance and brokenness. I was discipling everyone else's children and neglecting my own.

Mark Holmen writes, "As I've talked with pastors, many have confessed that they don't take the time to pray with their families or lead their families in Bible reading or devotions. Many have said, 'I deal with that at work all day and I don't have the time or energy to do it at home.'" That was me. I was investing everything into my spiritual opportunities at church, while neglecting my spiritual responsibilities to disciple my wife and children at home. Thankfully, it was not too late for me! God finally turned my heart (see Mal. 4:6) to the primary ministry and mission of my family.

The past seven years have been transformational. God has increasingly given me the grace to put first things first by ministering to my wife and six children. Personal repentance quickly spread to pastoral repentance. I had little understanding, and even less conviction, that God calls parents to be the primary spiritual trainers of their children. I didn't know that it was not my job as a pastor to disciple kids at church but rather to equip their parents to disciple them at home.

Would you like to see parents take the lead in passing faith to their children at home, for the glory of God and for the generations to come? Then make a central part of the mission of your church to equip them for this task. Precious few adults in your church grew up in homes that practiced family worship. Even fewer were thoroughly discipled by a parent. You not only need to tell parents and grandparents that they ought to do this, but you must also equip them with how to do it. The Faith@Home approach can help lead your church from a program-driven, church-building-centered church to a discipleship-driven, home-and-community impacting church.

This is not a quick fix. If you want to lead your church to reclaim a biblical vision for faith at home, be prepared for Satan to throw everything at you. Be strong and courageous.

Consider Mark's challenge: "Of all the things that you can do as a leader in Christ's church, there is nothing more important than helping bring Christ and Christlike living into the center of every home."

Nearly every time I muster the courage to set both of my feet—along with the rest of my body—on a scale, the reading ends up being completely different than what I expect. Watching my weight and following good eating habits never used to be an issue for me. But now that I'm past age 40, I've learned that something strange occurs with men and their metabolism during their middle-aged years.

I'm amazed at how quickly I can now gain 5, 10 and even 15 pounds when I simply enjoy the food I used to eat as a young adult. When I was younger, a few vigorous workouts at the gym over several days easily took care of that extra weight. Unfortunately, that's no longer the case. You wouldn't believe the number of times during the past year I've jumped into a major workout routine in an attempt to lose that extra 10 or 15 pounds.

I head off to the health club for a couple of hours each day to run on the treadmill, ride an exercise bike, work the elliptical trainer and then sit in the sauna. During this time, I'm completely confident that my rigorous and sweat-laden routine will certainly take care of my spare weight, just as it did in my younger years.

At the end of the week, I'm fully prepared to see the results of my hard work. So I slowly step on the scale. To my amazement, I discover that I haven't lost 5, 10 or even 15 pounds. Instead, I've gained half a pound! At this point, I become completely unglued Yet in the middle of my "Are you kidding me?" rant, I remember the words my wife, Maria (who, incidentally, has lost more than 60 pounds and looks better at 40 than she did when she was 20, which is completely unfair), has been saying to me: "Honey, you're not 20 anymore. If you want to lose weight, you're going to have to take a serious look at your eating habits."

What I was trying to accomplish—eating anything I want to eat and then working out a few days to take the pounds back off—simply wasn't working. The proof was in the extra weight I was carrying around. I didn't want to face this reality, yet I knew that if I didn't confront this ever-growing problem, it would only get worse.

Families in Crisis

Have you ever been in a situation like my battle of the bulge in which the true results ended up being completely different from what you thought they would be? I wonder if that's how the Pharisees felt when they expended their best efforts to thwart the movement that Jesus was leading. The apostle John records what these religious leaders did when they realized that something wasn't working: "Then the chief priests and the Pharisees called a meeting of the Sanhedrin. 'What are we accomplishing?' they asked" (John 11:47).

Notice the Pharisees focused on one question: *What are we accomplishing?* In spite of their efforts to stop Jesus, He was gaining popularity and momentum. The religious leaders of the day faced some difficult realities caused by Jesus. From their perspective, if they didn't deal with these realities, they faced some major short-term and long-term problems.

In a similar way, as pastors and church leaders we face a difficult reality that we must confront today. If we don't confront this problem, it will only get worse and we will end up facing even greater short-term and long-term issues. This problem lies at the core of many of the issues facing the Church, yet many church leaders spend little or no time addressing it and continue to go on with business as usual. While they might occasionally preach a sermon about this problem or dedicate a special evening to it, they haven't truly addressed it.

So, what problem am I talking about? Let me see if I can sum it up in 10 words or less: *Faithful Christlike living isn't happening in our homes today.*

The Heart of the Problem

In other words, families of all shapes and sizes aren't applying faith or biblical living to their everyday lives at home.

Over the past few years I have had the privilege to travel around the world and speak to thousands of church leaders, and the one thing that has truly amazed me is the way that the Faith@Home message is embraced and needed everywhere I go. It doesn't matter whether I am speaking to denominational or non-denominational church leaders, large-church or small-church leaders, German, Norwegian, Canadian, Swedish or Dutch leaders—they all recognize that building faith in the home is one of their greatest issues and needs. Gary Schwammelein, International Director of the Willow Creek Association, which has over 20 international outlets, says, "Your Faith@Home presentations and ministry ideas have been one of the highest rated we have had anywhere." Why is this?

As church leaders, we need to face the fact that no matter what size or expression of church we serve, the people who come to our churches are not engaging in faithful living at home. When it comes to talking about faith, praying, reading the Bible or engaging in any type of service or worship in the home, these practices simply aren't happening. Search Institute conducted a nationwide survey of over 11,000 participants from 561 congregations across six different denominations. The results are revealing:

- Only 12 percent of youth have a regular dialog with their mother on faith and/or life issues.
- Only 5 percent of youth have a regular dialog with their father on faith and/or life issues.
- Only 9 percent of youth have experienced regular reading of the Bible and devotions in the home.
- Only 12 percent of youth have experienced a servanthood event with a parent as an action of faith.[2]

George Barna confirmed this in his research for his book *Transforming Children into Spiritual Champions:*

We discovered that in a typical week, fewer than 10 percent of parents who regularly attend church with their kids read the Bible together, pray together (other than at mealtimes) or participate in an act of service as a family unit. Even fewer families—1 out of every 20—have any type of worship experience together with their kids, other than while they are at church during a typical month.[3]

So, as you can see, *faithful, Christlike living isn't happening in our homes today.* The result is a crisis with both short-term and long-term consequences.

The short-term consequences are being seen in a variety of ways. For instance, Christians fare no better than non-Christians when it comes to divorce, alcohol abuse, drug abuse and addiction to pornography. Clearly, the fact that Christlike living is not happening in homes today is having an immediate impact. The long-term consequences are revealed in current statistics that come from a variety of sources:

- If current trends in the belief systems and practices of the younger generation continue, in 10 years, church attendance will be half the size it is today.[4]
- Sixty-one percent of today's young adults had been churched at one point during their teen years, but they are now spiritually disengaged.[5]
- The Southern Baptist Convention reports that they are currently losing 70 to 88 percent of the young people after their freshman year in college . . . and the young people may never come back.[6]
- In one study, 90 percent of youth active in high school church programs drop out of church by their second year of college.[7]

Based on these statistical findings, anywhere from 60 to 90 percent of the children enrolled in your church programs today are going to disengage from the Christian faith when they are young adults. Clearly, something isn't working.

Satan's Strategy

Our enemy, Satan, is continually at work to stop Christianity from advancing, and it has become clear over the last few decades that Satan has moved his emphasis to the home. Satan realizes that he will not prevail against the Church because Jesus has already declared that he will not: "I tell you that you are Peter, and on this rock I will build my church, and the gates of Hades will not overcome it" (Matt. 16:18). Yet no such promise regarding the home was made; therefore, Satan realizes that the home is open territory for him to go to work. And during the last 40 to 50 years, Satan has been at work to take Christ and Christlike living out of the home because he realizes that if he can accomplish this, he can impact the advance of Christianity not only for today but also for generations to come.

When author David Kinnaman studied what 18- to 29-year-olds thought of Christianity for his book *UnChristian*, one of the things he discovered was that the majority of them felt Christianity was hypocritical. Eighty-five percent of young people who are not Christians have had sufficient exposure to Christians and churches to conclude that present-day Christianity is hypocritical. This negative perception has been similarly expressed by young churchgoers: Almost half agreed that Christianity is hypocritical (47 percent).[8]

Many 18- to 29-year-olds believe Christianity is hypocritical because the version of Christianity they experienced was something that was "done" only at church and not at home. I refer to it as a different version of a drug problem. On Sunday mornings, many of these 18- to 29-year-olds were "drug" to church where they were put into church programs, but when they went home, there was no faith talk, prayer, Bible reading or any other form of Christian living. So for them, Christianity was just something where you act, dress and behave one way at church and then go home and act, dress and behave completely different. Whether we like it or not, in most young people's experience, the term "hypocritical" has become fused with Christianity. As a result, many of these 18- to 29-year-olds are walking away from Christianity, looking for "real" spirituality.

Friends, Christianity was never meant to be "at church" focused. The Christian faith has always been meant to be a 24/7 lifestyle. Satan, however, has been at work for generations to get us to be one-hour-at-church-only Christians because he realizes that by doing this, he can slowly and methodically lead generations of people away from Christianity.

The Most Important Place

In Deuteronomy 6:3-7, Moses states, "Hear, O Israel, and be careful to obey so that it may go well with you and that you may

increase greatly in a land flowing with milk and honey, just as the
Lord, the God of your fathers, promised you. Hear, O Israel: The
Lord our God, the Lord is one. Love the Lord your God with all
your heart and with all your soul and with all your strength. These
commandments that I give you today are to be upon your hearts.
Impress them on your children. Talk about them (the commands
of God) when you sit at home and when you walk along the road,
when you lie down and when you get up. Tie them as symbols on
your hands and bind them on your foreheads. Write them on the
doorframes of your houses and on your gates."

Did you see where God intends faith to be nurtured? At home!
The home has always been intended by God to be the primary
place where faith is lived, discussed and nurtured. And research
confirms that what happens in the home is more influential than
what happens at church. I remember when I was confronted with
this reality.

In my early years as a youth and family pastor, I was satisfied
if I had a lot of teenagers involved in our youth programs. I
thought I was doing my job if I reached teens for Christ, got them
involved in church programs, and took them on youth trips and
to Bible camp. One day, I received a questionnaire to give to the
teenagers in my youth group. The survey was titled "The Most Significant Religious Influences."[9] This national survey was conducted by the Search Institute to help determine what factors
influenced teens in their faith.[10]

I strategically gave the questionnaire to my students after we'd
been on a youth trip together, hoping to increase my score as their
youth pastor. As instructed, I collected the surveys and returned
them to the Search Institute. It took months to get the results, but
I still remember receiving the envelope stamped with the words
"Survey Results Inside." I was on my way to a youth board meeting, and I thought this would be the opportunity of a lifetime. I
was certain that the results would show that I, the esteemed youth
and family pastor, was the top influence in the faith journey of
our church's youth. I even wondered if these results would
strengthen my case for a raise.

Mainline Protestant Youth Most Significant Religious Influences*

MOST SIGNIFICANT RELIGIOUS INFLUENCES	Percent Choosing as One of Top 5							
	GRADE						GENDER	
	7th	8th	9th	10th	11th	12th	M	F
Mother	87	75	77	72	75	75	81	74
Father	64	51	55	49	57	51	61	50
Grandparent	36	28	29	34	27	22	30	29
Another relative	11	12	14	16	12	7	13	12
Siblings	22	14	13	13	15	14	18	14
Friends	22	24	28	25	31	31	22	29
Pastor	60	56	49	45	36	49	57	44
Church camp	23	30	26	25	23	23	20	28
Movie/music star	3	3	4	4	2	2	4	3
Christian Education at my church	23	30	25	25	31	25	26	26
Church school teacher	29	27	17	23	20	23	26	21
Youth Group at my church	25	25	32	33	33	34	30	30
Youth Group Leader at my church	13	11	20	17	17	15	15	16
Youth Group outside my church	3	6	2	3	4	5	4	4
Youth Group Leader outside my church	2	1	1	3	4	4	2	3
The Bible	25	30	27	23	16	26	24	25
Other books I have read	2	3	4	4	3	4	3	4
Prayer of meditation	9	15	15	16	20	18	11	19
School teacher	3	5	2	2	3	6	3	4
Revivals or rallies	3	3	4	4	5	4	3	4
TV or radio evangelist	2	·	1	·	·	·	1	1
Worship services at church	10	10	10	16	14	15	12	13
God in my life	3	3	11	11	13	13	8	13
Work camp	·	1	4	2	5	5	3	3
Mission study tour	0	0	·	0	1	1	·	·
Retreats	7	12	16	20	17	18	11	17
Coach	2	2	3	3	4	4	4	2
Choir or music at church	11	12	8	9	11	6	7	12

*Includes mainline Protestant youth only (CC, ELCA, PCUSA, UCC, UMC) weighted by congregational and denomination size.

At the youth board meeting, I opened the letter and began to read the results. The most significant religious influence for Christian teens today is . . . Mom. At first I was upset, but then I quickly rationalized that no one can compete with moms. So I moved on.

The second most significant religious influence for Christian teens today is . . . Dad. This one hurt. I'd been around most of the dads of the teens in my youth group, and I knew that I spent more time with their kids than they did! How could dads possibly be more influential than I was?

My heart continued to sink as significant religious influence number three was a grandparent, followed by friends and siblings. "Youth group leader at my church" was way down the list. At that point, I accepted the reality that parents are the primary influences in the faith development of children.

In *Soul Searching*, Christian Smith summarizes, "Most teenagers and their parents may not realize it, but a lot of research in the sociology of religion suggests that the most important social influence in shaping young people's religious lives is the religious life modeled and taught to them by their parents."[11]

The home—and what Mom and Dad do or don't do in the home—will always be more influential than the church when it comes to faith formation. In *Family, the Forming Center*, Marjorie Thompson writes, "For all their specialized training, church professionals realize that if a child is not receiving basic Christian nurture in the home, even the best teachers and curriculum will have minimal impact. Once-a-week exposure simply cannot compete with daily experience where personal formation is concerned."[12]

How Did We Get Here?

How did we get to the place where faith is not being lived out at home? Let me take you back to a warning we received in Deuteronomy 6:10-12: "When the Lord your God brings you into the land he swore to your fathers, to Abraham, Isaac and Jacob, to give you—a land with large, flourishing cities you did not build, houses filled with all kinds of good things you did not provide, wells you did not dig, and vineyards and olive groves you did not plant—then when you eat and are satisfied, be careful that you do not forget the Lord."

I think there are two answers to my initial question. First, as individuals who live in a land of plenty where there is plenty to do, have, be and achieve, we have gotten caught up doing more, having more, being more and achieving more, and as a result we have forgotten God. Second, when we either don't have the time or forget altogether to fulfill a responsibility, our solution is to have someone else do it for us. If we don't have time to cook a family meal, we go out to a restaurant and have someone else do the cooking for us. When we don't have time to change the oil in our car, we go to a drive-through oil-change service. When we don't have time to clean the house, we hire a cleaning person to come in once a week. And when we don't have time to teach our kids about God, we take them to church and expect the church to do it for us. And if our kids don't seem to be "getting it," we leave that church and go to another one with a bigger, better children's or youth ministry program.

As church leaders, we need to remind our people that faith is not something they "do" at church or something that they have the experts "do" for them. The Christian faith is about living in a loving relationship with God—Father, Son and Holy Spirit—24 hours a day, 7 days a week.

I also think the same warning applies to the church that works in the land of plenty. We need to not get so caught up in the business of "doing" church that we place the focus on offering more programs to get more people, which then leads us to build bigger places; and then, since we now have more room, we can do more programs to get more and more people, which leads to . . . The wheel goes round and round. We have to be careful that we don't forget that what happens in the home is more influential than what happens at the church. We must be careful not to forget that we are called to equip the home for a lifestyle of faith. It is the home that is to be the primary place where faith is lived, expressed and nurtured.

My father was a youth and family pastor during the 1960s and 1970s, and during that time, the Church saw an explosion in Christian education through Sunday School and youth group ministries. Churches added education wings and youth rooms to their facilities, and these programs brought a lot of excitement to the Church. At the same time, families began to get busier as we moved out of the industrial age and into the technological age. Work schedules increased and more moms started working. When the Church began offering ministries for children and teenagers, parents welcomed the opportunity to bring their kids to church for a time of Christian education and fun. (Quite honestly, for many parents, this also provided a needed break from their children.)

While everyone's intentions were good, the Church failed to realize that many parents saw these programs as an opportunity to pass on the faith-nurturing responsibilities to the Church. Parents dropped off their kids and said, "Here you go—teach my children faith. I'll be back in an hour to pick them up."

Of course, the Church never intended for these programs to take the place of parents in the faith development of children. However, intentional or not, over the last 40 to 50 years, we've moved away from the home being the primary place where faith is nurtured. Researcher George Barna notes, "A majority of churches are actually guilty of perpetuating an unhealthy and unbiblical process wherein the church usurps the role of the family and creates an unfortunate sometimes exclusive dependency upon the church for a child's spiritual nourishment."[13]

Just as parents take their children to a soccer coach to learn soccer and to a piano teacher to learn piano, they bring their children to the local church to learn faith. This drop-off approach might, at best, keep kids busy in a church for a few years. But it usually doesn't lead to lasting faith that will stay with them through adolescence and into their adult years. Peter Benson notes:

Teaching values through programs is useful, but it is secondary in impact to how cultures have always passed on the best of human wisdom: through wisdom modeled, articulated, practiced, and discussed by adults with children around them. It is learning through engagement with responsible adults that nurtures value development and requires intergenerational community. Programs are an important reinforcement, but they are not the primary process.[14]

Lasting faith is a lifestyle that must be "caught" at home. It is not something that is simply taught at a church.

Faith that Doesn't Stick

Eddie was a perfect example of a child whose faith didn't stick. He was involved in every youth program we had. He came to every youth night, attended every retreat and summer camp we offered, and became a leader in our youth program. Yet we never saw his parents except when they picked him up or dropped him off at church. At one retreat, I asked him about his parents and he said, "They don't believe in Jesus, but they think church is a safe place for me to hang out. So that's why they let me stay involved in church."

When Eddie graduated from high school, he didn't have the money to attend college. So he worked. For a while, he stayed around church to help out with the youth program. But gradually, we saw less and less of him. About eighteen months after graduating from high school, Eddie was picked up for drunk driving. And that was just the beginning of a series of problems Eddie would have.

Eddie hasn't set foot in church for years. It makes me wonder how a leader of a church youth group—someone who clearly demonstrated a strong personal faith in Christ—could end up abandoning the faith and end up in jail just a few years later. I believe the answer is that his faith was never firmly "impressed" on and in him. His faith wasn't grounded at home. In fact, something else was impressed on Eddie. His dad was an alcoholic and began to buy Eddie alcohol after his high school graduation, even though he was underage. And Eddie's mom didn't really care if he continued going to church or not. Due to the influence Eddie received in his home, faith looked like a program rather than a lifestyle to him. And when the program was done, so was Eddie.

You've probably heard before what I'm about to say. But I hope that if you remember nothing else from this book, you'll remember this: *Faith is not something that can be taught; faith is something that must be caught.*

It's like catching a cold. When my daughter, Malyn, catches a cold at school and brings the virus into our home, what happens? That's right—inevitably, Maria and I also catch the cold! That's how faith works, too. When faith is in the home, everyone catches it! As pastors and leaders of Christ's church, we should be doing everything we can to get faith talk and living back into the homes and everyday life of the people of our churches. We must reestablish the home as the primary place where faith is nurtured.

What Does It All Mean?

The Bible makes clear (and research confirms) that the home is the primary place where faith must be nurtured. Both Scripture and research conclude that parents are the most important influences in passing on faith to children. So these truths beg the question: *Why do we focus almost all of our time, energy and resources on what takes place at church?*

In other words, if religious life in the home influences the faith of children more than what happens at church, and if parents are two to three times more influential than any church program, shouldn't we be investing the majority of our time and resources on equipping the home to be the primary place for nurturing faith?

When I was confronted with this information and this reality, I had a choice to make: I could continue leading and offering programs at church that would keep me and the people who attended our church very busy, or I could reexamine everything our church did through a set of lenses that focus on the question, "How can we reestablish the home as the primary place where faith is nurtured through our existing ministry structures?"

What I'm *Not* Saying

Before you read on, I need you to know that I do not believe we need to throw out the baby with the bathwater and eliminate or completely change worship, Sunday School, men's and women's ministry, Vacation Bible School, youth ministry, camps, retreats, and so on. I've personally experienced just how effective and critical these programs can be when it comes to passing on faith to children, youth and adults. Without them, we would certainly be in even bigger trouble. However, I do believe that we need to take a serious look at these ministries through a set of lenses that focus on equipping the home to be the primary place where faith is nurtured.

After a talk I recently gave, Sue Miller, longtime champion of making children's ministry the best hour out of the week for kids, stood before the audience of children's ministry leaders and said something I will never forget:

> Every time I hear Mark talk and see the statistics where children's ministry only rates at 25 percent, I always find myself getting a little agitated, wondering, is it worth it? Are you saying all this effort we put into making children's ministry the best hour out of the week for kids is only getting us to 25 percent?! But then I realized that if we continue to make children's ministry the best hour out of the week *and* at the same time motivate and equip people to live out their faith at home which scores at 81 percent, that means we have 25 percent + 81 percent, which equals 106 percent!

I love Sue Miller because she was able to convey the heartbeat of Faith@Home in such a succinct and commonsense way. We still need church programs, but they need to be church + home focused. When we get that happening, then we will truly see success. The good news is that to achieve success, we don't need to blow up the church or make some big shift or 180-degree turn. All we need are some two-degree shifts.

John Trent shared with me the two-degree principle, which can easily be understood using the following example. Imagine that we wanted to fly a rocket ship to the moon. To get our rocket to the moon, we would need to put in all the coordinates necessary to get us there. However, if those coordinates were off by just two degrees, would we hit the moon? The answer is no. In fact, we wouldn't even hit Mars! Being two degrees off, which doesn't seem like much, when carried out over a long time or a great distance leads us farther and farther off course.

Because we as churches, as well as individuals, have not been Faith@Home focused for many generations now, the results show that we are significantly off course. Yet through the Faith@Home movement, we have the ability to make two-degree changes that will get us back on course in our ministries. These two-degree changes are not only necessary for our good and that of the current generation, but they will also have huge ramifications for our grandchildren and their children.

Problems We All Face

I hope that you're beginning to realize that the playing field has been leveled. Regardless of the size of church we serve, when it comes to equipping people to apply faith and biblical living to their everyday lives at home, we all face the same difficult realities. To confirm this, let's look at some common problems confronting us.

Problem 1: Declining Engagement

One common symptom of a program-driven faith is that as age increases, attendance and participation decline. Dawson McAlister, a national youth ministry specialist, says, "Ninety percent of kids active in high school youth groups do not go to church by the time they are sophomores in college. One third will never return."[15]

In the typical American program-driven church, it's considered normal to see a decline in participation of programs as children grow older. It's not unusual for a church to have 40 students per class when the children are ages 5 to 10, but then see the numbers decline to 20 students per class when they reach ages 11 to 15, and only 10 students per class when they reach ages 16 to 18.

Most churches rationalize this decline with statements such as, "Kids today are so busy with other activities that they just don't have time for church." My response to that is simple: "You're probably right. They don't have time for another program. But faith isn't supposed to be about a program. It's supposed to be about a relationship, and relationships get stronger and more committed over time. If the youth in your church are disengaging over time, you probably have a Faith@Home problem, because they are involved in the programs for as long as they like the programs; but they are not living in relationship, because when the programs change, many of them disengage. You don't disengage from relationships that matter to you, but you do disengage from programs when they no longer appeal to you."

Maria and I have the privilege of being in a small group with four other families. Each has made a commitment to bring Christ and Christlike living into the center of their homes. Together, we have 10 adults and 12 kids ranging in ages from 8 to 16. I've noticed that as our children get older, none of them is any less involved in church. If anything, they're becoming more involved and more committed—to the point that they sometimes drag us to church events! I believe that the teenagers have seen their parents actively involved in a personal relationship with Jesus Christ, which influences the decisions they make and the activities they're involved in. As a result, these teenagers are following in their parents' footsteps of faith.

Why don't some teenagers stay engaged in their faith? Because for many, faith was really nothing more than a program they attended. As they got older and wiser, they started to see faith as hypocritical, because their parents acted one way at church and a completely different way at home. Then when these teenagers became young adults, they concluded, "If that's what Christianity is about, I don't want anything to do with it."

If we want our children to have a faith that influences the way they live and the critical life decisions they make, then we need to be modeling faith through a personal relationship with Jesus Christ in our homes. We shouldn't simply write off declining attendance and participation as "normal" or because "kids today are so busy." It's not normal! It's a symptom of the problem we face, and it needs to be addressed.

Problem 2: Drop-off Mentality

As I mentioned earlier, for many families today, the church is sometimes no more than a safe "drop-off center" for kids. Not long ago, Maria was reading a magazine article as she ran on the treadmill. The article gave readers ideas about how they could add 30 minutes to their day. The last suggestion almost made her fall off the treadmill. One woman proudly stated that she'd found a way to get two hours more out of her week by dropping her kids off at church and running errands while they were in Sunday school! Why not? After all, the church is a place that will teach children good morals, keep them out of trouble, and surround them with other good kids their age.

At Ventura Missionary Church, where I served as senior pastor for seven years, we had an elementary school that started with kindergarten and went through eighth grade. Some 40 percent of the students who attended our school came from unchurched families. Most of these parents were hardworking people who made a significant financial sacrifice to enroll their children in our private school. Each weekday morning, these parents would pull into our parking lot and drop off their children with the expectation that we would teach them good morals and solid faith. Yet when we urged parents to be a part of teaching these same morals and faith to their children at home, they often dug in their heels and said, "That's what we pay you to do."

Of course, it's easy to see how this happens in a private school situation. But if you don't think it also happens in your children's and youth programs, you simply have blinders on. Many of the people who enroll their children and youth in your church programs do so with the same drop-off expectations. I don't think this was God's intention when He created the Church.

I agree with researcher George Barna when he writes in *Transforming Children into Spiritual Champions*, "The local church should be an intimate and valuable partner in the effort to raise the coming generation of Christ's followers and church leaders, but it is the parents whom God will hold primarily accountable for the spiritual maturation of their children."[16]

When I would lead a new member class at our church, I would be pretty blunt in stating that if people were looking for a church where they could drop off their children and expect us to teach them faith, we weren't the right church for them. Of course, I added that we would gladly come alongside them and partner with them to bring Christ and Christlike living into the center of their homes. If that's what they're looking for, we would gladly welcome them into our community.

Problem 3: Loss of Standing

Many families today don't recognize the Church as a resource that can help them with their family relationships. They will quickly turn to TV and radio shrinks, the Internet, counseling and even medication to help them as a family, but the Church isn't even a blip on their radar.

One time, I worked with a family who had been through an ugly divorce. The parents battled almost every situation through lawsuits and court cases. They tried counseling but quit out of frustration. As is often the case, the children found themselves continually in the middle of their parents' warfare.

I became involved in the situation because the teenage daughter, Abby, started attending our youth worship service through the invitation of a school friend. Eventually, Abby joined a small group and began to open up. Things hit rock bottom one Friday night when she came to church and asked to meet with me. She informed me that her mom was home drunk because she had just had another fight with her ex-husband. Abby didn't know what to do, so we called her mom and got permission for her to stay at her friend's house that night.

The next day, I went over to meet with Abby's mom. When I arrived, I was greeted rather abruptly. "Who are you and what do you want?" she said.

"My name is Pastor Mark," I said as politely as I could. "Abby is part of our youth group, and I was wondering if we could talk for a minute."

I could tell by her reaction that she was somewhat surprised and a bit ashamed. "I'm sorry," she responded more softly, "I thought you were a door-to-door salesman." She invited me in, and after a few minutes I informed her that Abby had told me about the ugly divorce and the drinking problem she had. I asked if there was anything I could do to help.

The look of brokenness in her eyes said it all as she struggled to reply. I looked her in the eyes and said softly, "Ma'am, I'm not here to judge you or to preach to you. I just want you to know that you, your children and even your ex-husband matter to God. We would welcome the opportunity to show you how Christ wants to help you and your family."

She then broke into tears, and after a few moments she replied, "I used to go to church before all this happened. But after all of this mess, I thought church was only for families who had it all together and that I was no longer welcome."

Over the course of the next two years, we were able to come alongside this family and see God work many miracles. Abby now attends a Christian college and is studying to be a youth pastor. Her mom made a complete turnaround and is now remarried to a wonderful Christian man.

While Abby's story is great news, the point I'm trying to make is that the Church needs to get back on the radar for families. If it hadn't been for Abby, her mom probably would never have set foot in a church during her time of crisis and need. Whether she was right or wrong, she had pegged the Church as a place only for families that are healthy and put together. The Church needs to break that stereotype and put out a welcome mat that reads, "*All* families are welcome here"!

Problem 4: Ill-equipped Parents.
A while back, I was speaking to a group of parents and teenagers. I began my talk by asking a series of questions.

"Raise your hand if you think you could name one of the 12 disciples." Nearly every hand in the room went up.

"Raise your hand if you could name a living disciple today." Just a few hands went up.

"Raise your hand if you believe in Jesus Christ as your Lord and Savior." Again, every hand went up.

I then told the teenagers and parents to look at each other, and made the following statement: "Realize that the person you're looking at—who stated he or she believes in Jesus Christ as Lord and Savior—is a disciple of Jesus Christ." The crowd began to murmur a little. From the front row, one boy pointed his finger at his dad and loudly proclaimed, "No way—not *him!*" The boy wanted to go on to tell all the ways his father wasn't a disciple of Christ! Obviously, this wasn't the point of the exercise, but it did make for a powerful illustration. Our children are watching us to see if our behaviors reflect the faith we proclaim.

Many parents today would rather pass instilling their children's faith on to the "professionals" at church instead of tackling this responsibility themselves. Because they often didn't experience what it was like to have Christ as a part of the home they grew up in, they don't have a model to follow. As each generation becomes less and less involved in the Christian Church—and, as a result, with faith at home—more and more parents are now two to three generations removed from the last generation that remembers having faith talk, Bible reading, devotions and prayer in the home.

Talk to the parents in your church and you'll find that they have a desire to bring "spirituality," as they might call it, into the home. But they have absolutely no idea how to do this, because they never experienced these matters of faith in their home when they were growing up. Even the strongest families in your church might surprise you with their lack of ability to talk with their children about faith or even a willingness to pray together as a family.

The Thompson family in my church was a perfect example of this. One day, Alan Thompson, an active member of our congregation, called my office. While he often chatted with me at church, he rarely called. I immediately presumed something was wrong.

He stammered a bit, searching for the right words, and then said, "I'm having troubles with my 15-year-old, Andrea."

"What do you mean by 'troubles'?" I asked.

"We're not communicating real well, and it seems like we're always on opposite ends of every situation. I'd like to talk with you to see if there is anything I can do so that we're not always fighting."

Realizing that he needed more than a quick answer over the phone, I decided to go visit the family at their home. Alan, his wife and two children lived in a beautiful home. By the world's standards, they appeared to have everything together. Alan was involved in a variety of committees at church, and his wife helped out with Sunday School. Andrea was actively involved in the youth ministry and also helped teach Sunday School.

When I arrived, Alan invited me in and we sat down to talk in the living room. For the first 30 minutes, he shared story after story with me of how disrespectful Andrea had become. "She doesn't listen to me anymore," he exclaimed. "Whenever I establish a rule or guideline, she always seems to push just beyond the limit. That forces me to have to do something about it. I'm also concerned about the friends she's hanging out with. I'm wondering if I need to limit how much time she can spend with them."

As Alan continued ticking off his concerns, I thought to myself, *What am I going to say? I don't have a teenager and I've never had to face this myself.* When he had finally exhausted himself of stories, he turned to me and said, "What am I supposed to do?"

Not wanting to let on that I actually felt ill-equipped to handle his family's situation, I did what I always try to do when I get in over my head: I turned to God for help. Then I sat back in the chair, turned to him and said, "Have you prayed with Andrea about this?"

This didn't seem like an outrageous question to me. I had seen Alan lead prayer many times at committee meetings, and his daughter led prayer in Sunday School every week. Yet the look in his eyes told me all I needed to know.

During the first 15 years of Andrea's life, Alan had been actively involved in taking her to daycare, soccer practice, piano lessons and even church. But he had never prayed with her. The idea of praying with his daughter for the first time as a teenager now seemed utterly beyond the scope of reason.

Many parents share this feeling that they are ill equipped to lead their children in the faith. I once co-led a workshop with David Anderson called "Nurturing Faith of Teenagers." I set the stage by helping parents list and outline the characteristics and issues of teenagers today. Dr. Anderson then took it a step further by asking the parents, "How many of you here today wish your teenager had a stronger faith?" Every hand in the room went up. He then made a comment that I'll never forget: "While it's good that we all desire our teenagers have a stronger faith, the reality is that what we see in our teenagers' faith is simply a mirror image of our faith. So the issue is not their faith, but our faith."

As we noted earlier, Scripture clearly states that parents have both the responsibility and honor to pass on the faith to their children (see Deut. 6). Martin Luther put it this way: "Most certainly father and mother are apostles, bishops, and priests to their children, for it is they who make them acquainted with the gospel."[17] Think about that for a minute. Imagine if every parent in your church thought of themselves as a bishop, apostle and priest to their children. That's what I call a "home as church too" vision! However, for that vision to become a reality, we need to train and equip parents to be the bishops, apostles and priests in their own homes.

Problem 5: Competition

Another problem that we must face isn't actually a problem with the Church, but it's still a problem. It's the reality that families today have more things competing for their time than ever before. Whether or not we want to admit it, the Church is in competition with the world.

Jack Eggar, president and CEO of Awana Clubs International, once said, "There has never been a time in history when the children of the world have been more spiritually at risk than they are today. A plethora of competing worldviews and warped values flow freely throughout society—directly into the minds of children, where they stay for a lifetime."[18]

Just a few decades ago, the Church played a much more significant role in the lives of families. It wasn't unusual to see businesses closed on Sundays, and public schools wouldn't give homework on Wednesdays because that evening was "church night." Families were committed to being at church whenever the doors were open. And families frequently came together with other like-minded families who attended church for fellowship, fun and even vacation!

Some time ago, I had a chance to experience a "blast from the past" when I was asked to speak at Brown City Family Camp, one of the nation's largest family camps. This family camp, located on a 12-acre piece of property in northern Michigan, has been running for more than 75 years. The camp only opens for two weeks of family camp each year, and it draws more than 2,000 people from all over Michigan. These families spend an intense week eating together, worshiping together, singing together, playing together and shutting off all the noise from the outside world—that's right, no TVs, computers or cell phones—just to be with God and each other. The camp draws families with newborns to people over 90 years old, creating a truly multigenerational gathering. As I walked around and talked with people, there was one comment I heard repeatedly: "We wouldn't miss this family camp for anything. This is the best thing our family does every year."

Today, however, hardly any family would think of spending such an intense week or two with other Christian families. Few people even recognize the concept of "church night." Sunday morning is business as usual. If anything, the Church now competes with sports leagues and many other extracurricular activities that vie for the family's time—even on Sunday mornings. And one of the most common excuses I hear from Church leaders as to why people aren't attending their events at church is, "Our people are just so busy today; they don't have time to attend our event."

Let me reply to that as kindly as I can. That's just a bunch of hogwash! The people in our congregations *do* have time for the things that will truly help them be better moms, dads, husbands, wives, and so on. Unfortunately, we have been simply offering them entertaining programs at church instead of ministries that will actually help them bring Christ and authentic Christlike living back into their daily life. We are losing the competition time war not because we don't have something good to offer, but because we aren't offering the good life we have to offer.

Ponder, Pray and Discuss

1. Reflect on this statement: "What happens in the home is two to three times more influential than what happens at church when it comes to faith formation." Do you agree or disagree? Why?

2. Have you ever surveyed the people in your church to see what percentage of them . . .

   • Pray in the home?
   • Read the Bible at home?
   • Have engaged in any form of regular Christian service at home?
   • Have engaged in any form of worship at home?
   • Engage in some sort of faith talk with their mom at least once per month?
   • Engage in some sort of faith talk with their dad at least once per month?

   What do you think they would say? Reflect on your answer.

3. How does the statistical information regarding faith behaviors at home affect you and the church you serve?

CHAPTER SUMMARY

- There is competition for what will take the top priority in your ministry.

- As a pastor, you need to gain a passion for making faith at home ministry your top priority.

- Your legacy is to reestablish home as the primary place where faith is nurtured.

- Parents today are searching for a better way to "do family."

- God desires that families not just survive but also thrive.

- You need to become a pastor whose heart bleeds for families.

- The "God Things" that gave me a passion, a vision and a model for the Faith@Home movement.

- The struggle with making faith a priority in your own home.

- Bringing Christ back into the center of the home is about you and your passion and commitment.

- The blessings your family will enjoy when you bring Christ back into the center of your home.

- The blessings your church will enjoy when members bring Christ back to the center of their homes.

Do We Care?

I have never seen parents more hungry for help than they are now.
They want to spend more time with their children. They feel acutely the
need to be better equipped as parents.[1]
MARK DEVRIES

ANOTHER VOICE SAYS...

Mark Batterson, Pastor and Author
National Community Church, Washington, DC

When my oldest son turned 12, I created a discipleship covenant. Over the next year, I helped him accomplish intellectual, spiritual and physical challenges that I thought would help him grow in those areas. It was an amazing experience. Probably the most important thing I've done. I honestly believe that discipling my kids is far more important than pastoring National Community Church. NCC can find another pastor. But my kids can't find another dad. Nothing is more important or more challenging than discipling my kids. And I need all the help I can get. I'm so grateful for the Faith@Home focus! I think it helps reorder our priorities: God first, family second, church third.

I'll always remember the day I was talking with some fellow pastors in our community about the condition of families. I invited them to participate in a meeting that our church was hosting to discuss how local churches and pastors could work together to reclaim homes and families for Christ.

As I extended this invitation, the blank stares I received told me everything I needed to know. "That's not my thing," one pastor said to me. "I might send my children's pastor, but that's simply not something I have any interest in attending."

This kind of reaction isn't limited to the pastors in my community. A few years ago, George Barna conducted a series of day-long seminars across the country that covered four major issues facing the Church. One of the four sessions focused on the importance of children and family ministry. George had previously conducted similar one-day seminars on different topics, but with this series, something happened that he had never seen before. Instead of simply registering for the all-day seminar, numerous pastors called his office and said, "I'm planning to come to your seminar, but could you tell me when the session on children and family ministry will take place? I don't plan to go to that part of the seminar. In fact, I would like to send my children's pastor to that session."

When it comes to the issue of equipping families to apply faith or biblical living in their everyday lives at home, my heart breaks every time I hear a pastor say, "That's not my thing" or "That's for the children's pastor." I simply can't understand why, as pastors and leaders, we wouldn't want to make Faith@Home a top priority in our churches.

I'll admit that until I became a senior pastor, I had no idea how many voices would be calling for me to make various ministries and programs a top priority in the church. The latest prayer magazine arrives and makes a compelling argument that we need to be a church fully committed to prayer. Then a worship magazine comes along stating the importance of making worship top priority. Then an email alerts me to the latest stewardship seminar we need to host because stewardship is the key to the blessings that God wants to pour out in our church. Then I receive a full-color brochure about a missional-living conference urging us to get more engaged in our community. I place that on my desk next to the Purpose Driven Life conference and the small-groups conference that I should be attending. Oh, and global missions Sunday is coming up, and we need to be a church that goes out into all nations to reach people for Christ!

Am I the only one who's overwhelmed and confused?

Where's Your Heart?

I'm guessing that these and other tensions and tugs also demand your time, attention and resources. Yet somehow, here you are reading this book. That means you must have some interest and passion for seeing Christ and Christlike living in the center of every home. With that in mind, how do you feel when you read the following statements from George Barna's research?

- A large majority of believers rely on their church, rather than on their families, to train their children to become spiritually mature.
- In an average month, fewer than 1 out of every 10 churched families worship together outside of a church service. Just as few pray together, other than at mealtimes, and the same minimal numbers study the Bible together at home or work together to address the needs of the disadvantaged people in their community.
- The likelihood of a married couple who are born-again churchgoers getting divorced is the same as couples who are not disciples of Jesus.
- Apart from church-based programs, the typical Christian family spends less than 3 hours per month in endeavors designed to jointly develop or apply their faith.
- Most Christian parents do not believe they are doing a good job at facilitating the spiritual development of their children.[2]

How do these statements make you feel? How do they affect your approach to ministry? As Satan intentionally and methodically takes Christ and Christlike living out of our homes, my question to you as a fellow pastor and leader in God's church is simply, "Do you care?"

Of Course You Care!

Please hear me when I say that I know you care. You wouldn't be in ministry unless you cared about Christ, His Church and His people. I know that lost people matter to you because they matter to Christ. You wouldn't put yourself on the front lines of ministry day after day if you didn't care. In fact, one of the things I emphasize when I speak at conferences across the world is that senior pastors *do* care about this. It's not that we don't want people to be faith-at-home focused!

Yet, as a former senior pastor, one thing I'm asking you to prayerfully consider is the fact that maybe in our pursuit to grow our churches, we might have lost sight of what's happening in the homes of our church members. Perhaps we need to care a little less about the programs people try to pressure us into making top priority in our churches so we can care more about what's happening in the homes and families of the people in our churches. I want to personally challenge you, just as God challenged me. Of all the things you can do as a leader in Christ's church, there is nothing more important than helping to bring Christ and Christlike living into the center of every home.

As a pastor, what do you want your legacy to be? What does success look like to you? Will it just be building a large congregation and a big and beautiful facility? Or will it be equipping people to live out their faith at home so that we don't lose the following generations from the faith?

Here's Your Chance

I love the Church, and I believe that God is calling the Church to rise up and address the area that Satan is attacking the most—our families. Through the years, my experience tells me that parents today want to have a better family than the one in which they grew up. They're searching for a better way to "do family." As youth and family pastor Mark DeVries writes, "In my fifteen years of youth ministry, I have never seen parents more hungry for help than they are now. They want to spend more time with their children. They feel acutely the need to be better equipped as parents."[3]

My friend Mike Engbers who launched the Faith@Home movement in his church writes, "One family in our church recently stopped me and asked if we had anything to help families teach their children faith in the home. We were able to say 'absolutely' and do a visit to their home to provide them with some of our resources. We've also seen families increase their commitment to church and reconnect with other families. We've seen the culture in our church starting to change where families are seeking support and guidance as they journey through life."

I firmly believe the Christian Church can offer what every household needs to succeed—a personal, growing relationship with Jesus Christ, who knocks at the door of their home and says, "Let Me in, and I'll help your family enjoy long life!" Now is the time for churches to come alongside families and equip them to bring Christ into the center of their homes. This could be our finest hour as the Church! As a pastor I served with once said to me, "The role of the Church isn't to make sure that, as you look down on this community, you can see the light shining bright from our facility. Rather, the role of the Church is to make sure the light shines in each and every home, lighting the community for the world to see!"

God Wants Families to Thrive!

The crisis that families face today isn't just an American problem. It's something pastors and leaders from all over the world must address. When my first book, *Faith Begins at Home,* was taken to a Christian publishing book fair in Germany, it was the most-requested book for translation into German. This was completely unexpected, because I was an unknown author. But I believe this happened because God is beginning to lead a movement to reclaim and reestablish families through His Church. And that's exciting!

Many parents today are searching for help. They want to succeed! They surf the Internet, watch *Oprah* and *Dr. Phil* and buy every self-help book that comes out in an effort to keep their families together for another day. Yet families seem to be hanging on by a thread. In our desperate search for answers, I wonder if we realize that God is there for families. In fact, He desires that families not just survive but also thrive!

The rest of this chapter might seem very personal to you. It is. I want to tell you my own story so that you can more fully understand for yourself how God is at work in leading this movement. I want to share with you some of the things God has done in my life to grow within me the Faith@Home passion and commitment that now drive me.

The "God Things" in My Life

I didn't always have the passion for building faith at home that I have today. To be honest, I spent a good part of my life without this issue even on my radar. My prayer in sharing this personal journey with you is for you to see how God has worked both in my life and in leading this movement. Everything that has occurred—the passion, the vision, the model and the Faith@Home movement—are about the Lord and not me. I don't deserve any of the credit. He deserves it all!

At a conference I spoke at recently, I was introduced as "a pastor whose heart bleeds for Faith@Home." As you read on, you'll see that a lot of "God things" had to take place in my life for this statement to be true. Perhaps God is calling you to be a part of the Faith@Home movement. If our churches are going to change, the change must begin with us as pastors and leaders. We must be personally convicted and passionate about this or nothing will change.

So what about you? Does your heart bleed for this?

God Thing #1: Bible Camp Living

Growing up as the son of a Bible camp director provided a unique—some of my friends would say warped—view on how to live for Christ. My family lived at the Bible camp, which meant I had a 500-acre backyard with hiking trails, soccer fields, softball diamonds, horseback riding, swimming, campfires, and a hundred new friends to play with every week! If I didn't like my friends one week, I knew I that I would get a hundred new ones the next week! My dad served as the executive director, and my mom worked in the office, helped in the kitchen and pretty much served as camp mom to the summer staff. My two older sisters also worked at the camp. Because they were 8 and 10 years older than I, they served as great role models for me.

Most people leave the real world for a spiritual refilling weekend or week at a camp or retreat. Once there, they tune out and leave behind the noise of the outside world and just spend time with God in His creation. At camp, everything focuses on Jesus— from the first thing you do in the morning until the last thing you do at night. But after a weekend or a week, you have to return home and go back to the daily grind.

For me, however, camp living was our real world. This meant that my family's lifestyle at home was pretty much 24/7 living for Christ. We prayed together as a family, went to worship and campfires together, sang Christian songs together, read the Bible together, served together and celebrated all the Christian holidays together. At camp, I saw what life was like when a person lived it completely for Christ. In contrast, church seemed boring to me. So, from a young age, I determined that I would be a camp director like my dad. I certainly didn't want to be a pastor!

During my four years at a Christian college, I worked at a different Bible camp each summer so that I could gain as much experience as possible. After graduation, I began my working career as the full-time program director for a Bible camp in Iowa. I was in my glory, as the camp provided an intentional Christian community where more than 3,000 people each year came for spiritual refueling.

Yet one thing disturbed me. Each week, we saw hundreds of kids get excited and passionate about their relationship with Jesus Christ. As they left camp, you could see the fire they had gained for living for Christ. But during the non-summer months when I preached in some of the congregations these campers came from, I could quickly see that the fire was no longer there. From my limited perspective, I realized that camp fired up kids for Christ while church seemingly served as a great fire extinguisher.

Although this bothered me, I wasn't too concerned because I was planning to always be a Bible camp director. So I didn't have to worry about the Church. At least, that's what I thought.

God Thing #2: Out of Camping Ministry and into the Church

During my fifth summer at this Bible camp, Maria and I went to a wedding in Minneapolis. Throughout the weekend, God seemed to be working in my heart with a new calling. On the drive back to Iowa, I suddenly asked Maria, "What would you think if we left camping ministry and pursued a calling to serve as a youth pastor in a church?"

I'll never forget her response—after the initial shock wore off: "You, Mr. Camp, the person who thinks camp is cool and church is boring, wants to leave camping to serve in a church?" As hard as it was for Maria to believe, it was equally terrifying for me. I had absolutely no congregational ministry experience! I didn't think any congregation would actually call a camp guy to serve their church, so I thought I was safe. Yet God guided us, and one church in a Minneapolis suburb patiently and persistently pursued me to come and serve as their associate minister overseeing youth and family ministry.

It didn't take long for me to realize the front-line nature of congregational ministry. I was constantly bombarded with the hurts and brokenness that occur in families. I began to see and experience firsthand what was happening in the Church. I observed how Satan strategically and methodically tears apart families, creating the pain, confusion and bitterness that turn family members away from God and each other.

Week after week, month after month, and year after year as I worked with people, God began to open my eyes. Prior to this experience, I often blamed the Church for putting out the fires for faithful living that God ignited at camp. But now I was confronted with the truth that the Church wasn't serving as the fire extinguisher—at least not directly.

In many ways, the Church did the same things we did at camp. Yet something was putting out those fires, and now I could see where the fire extinguisher was. It was the home! Christ and Christlike living clearly weren't happening in people's homes. For the first time, I understood that the type of home life I experienced growing up at camp was radically different than the life that existed in the majority of the families in our church. At this point, God began to break my heart and convict me that we had to do something to rescue families.

God Thing #3: A Mentor and a Child

I could now see the problem, but I didn't have a clue about a solution. At this point, God brought an important person into my life. His name was Dr. Dick Hardel. I had met Dick when I was in camping ministry, where he had spoken a few times at our youth retreats. At the time, he was an assistant to the bishop for the Nebraska synod of the Evangelical Lutheran Church in America. Each time he came to speak, it felt as if I had known him for a long time.

About the same time I accepted the call to leave camping ministry and come to the Minneapolis area, Dick had accepted a position as the director of the Youth and Family Institute in Minneapolis. When we ran into each other at a pastors' conference, we were like two long-lost friends who had been separated for years.

Dick had been a successful pastor for years, and he had always made faith at home a top priority in his ministry. Now he was bringing that passion to the Youth and Family Institute, where he could help congregations across the country partner with homes to pass on faith. Between the Institute's research and Dick's incredibly deep knowledge of Scripture and his contagious passion, I became compelled to put faith at home on my radar as a pastor.

As a result of our friendship, Dick and I began working together on ways we could bring Christ and Christlike living back into the home through existing church programs like Sunday School, youth groups and other ministries. Essentially, he was the "big idea" guy, while I served as the "practitioner." For the next 12 years, I had the privilege of serving in 3 congregations of different sizes (400, 1,200 and 2,500 worshipers). During those years, God began to develop a vision and a continually evolving model for a Faith@Home ministry that would transform the lives of families.

About the same time, God made the idea of family ministry even more personal for me. On October 31, 1995, my life changed forever. Maria and I found ourselves in a birthing room at North Memorial Hospital in Minneapolis. We had been married for five years at the time, but we now stood at the brink of becoming parents for the first time. For three hours, I steadfastly stood by Maria's side, serving as her focal point as she went through contraction after contraction. Then the incredible moment of truth arrived! Our daughter, Malyn, came into the world. What an amazing sight to see!

Immediately, the nurses whisked her away to the other side of the room to clean and measure her. Malyn was crying loudly, but Maria was also groaning from the pain of delivering her first child. To this day, I remember standing halfway between them wondering, *Which way do I go? Do I go to the side of my wife, who has just gone through one of the most exhausting and painful experiences of her life? Or do I go to the side of my precious little girl who is crying for the first time?*

Then the voice of God spoke to me—which, oddly, sounded a lot like Maria—and commanded, "Go make sure Malyn is okay." My daughter had been in the world for just 60 seconds, and as a parent I already needed help!

I'll never forget the first time I held this precious gift from God in my arms. I remember thinking, *Now what do I do?* I desperately wanted Malyn to know the love of Christ and to grow to love Jesus with all her heart, soul and strength. Yet we weren't living at a Bible camp, so we didn't have that environment to help us. I needed help, and I knew it! My work as a youth and family ministry pastor suddenly became intensely personal. It was as much for me as it was for anyone in the congregations I would serve.

God Thing #4: A Playground

Back in my college years, one of my best friends was a guy named Darel. He and I enjoyed playing basketball, golf, cards and pretty much anything competitive. We lived on the edge a bit, yet we always looked out for each other. After graduation, Darel met a young woman named Laura who quickly took hold of his heart. A couple of years later, he called and said that he and Laura were getting married, and he wanted me to help with the wedding.

Laura's dad, Steve, was the senior pastor of a fairly large church in Sioux City, Iowa. While he wanted to give the message for the wedding, he also wanted to just be the bride's dad for the rest of the service. I gladly agreed to take part, and on the weekend of the wedding, I had an opportunity to meet Steve as we worked through the ceremony. Steve was a great guy, and we had a lot of fun doing the service together. Yet little did I know that God had another purpose in mind.

About five years later, Steve took a call to serve as senior pastor of Calvary Lutheran Church in Golden Valley, Minnesota—one of the largest Lutheran churches in the nation. Steve's first task was to put together a new team of pastors to lead the ministry forward. One of the key positions was a pastor who would take charge of the entire children, youth and family ministry program at the church. This position meant overseeing a full-time staff of 12, a budget of nearly one million dollars, and programs that served approximately 1,500 children and youth.

Because of our previous encounter at Darel and Laura's wedding, Steve knew that I was a youth and family pastor. When he called and asked if I would consider interviewing for the position, I was both surprised and excited. Calvary was one of the leading congregations in youth and family ministry, and the opportunity to serve in a church of this size and with the resources they had was truly a dream opportunity. Following a series of interviews, Calvary offered me the opportunity to come and join their team. For five years, I was blessed to serve as their youth and family pastor.

Calvary was the greatest playground in the world for me. I had the opportunity to be creative and work with some of the most innovative leaders in youth and family ministry. Many years before I arrived, the church had made a commitment to being a faith at home congregation. While serving there, I was blessed to see how God could positively influence and change families when a church stuck with this commitment over an extended period of time.

Everything we did at Calvary with children, youth and families we did from the perspective of how it would affect the home. We watched as God truly transformed families. In addition, we began to have the opportunity to share our model with other congregations across the country. George Barna even contacted us and profiled us as an effective church in his book *Transforming Children into Spiritual Champions*.

God began to grow in me a desire to see other churches and church leaders infected with the passion to make faith at home a priority in their ministries. Now that I was in a church that was fully devoted to this model, I wanted other churches to experience the fruit that we were seeing. God had clearly been at work bringing together some of the most creative and innovative ideas through Dick Hardel and the Youth and Family Institute, with a driven practitioner like me, and a church with the resources and commitment to do whatever it takes to bring Christ and Christlike living into the home.

As a result, a conceptual model for a comprehensive and integrated Faith@Home ministry was birthed. Let me be clear: We didn't create a program. Rather, we created a conceptual model for how the Church needs to "do church" in order to reestablish the home as the primary place where faith can be nurtured. God was developing in me and in the churches I had the opportunity to work with a passion to look at everything we did through a set of lenses that focused on how everything that took place at church affected and equipped the home.

God Thing #5: A Senior Pastor's Perspective

Maria and I both thought I would serve at Calvary forever, but God wasn't done yet. He had even more that He wanted to do in and through us. I'll never forget the day that Pastor Steve gently asked if I had ever considered becoming a senior pastor. He wasn't trying to get rid of me—at least I don't think so. But he saw something in me that I didn't see myself. Up to that point, I had completely resisted the notion of becoming a senior pastor. I saw the toll that ministry often took on people and, frankly, I didn't want to run the risk of that happening to my family and me.

Steve invited me to attend a celebration marking the thirty-fifth anniversary of his ordination. I went because Darel and his family were there. During a program after the dinner, various people from Steve's previous churches spoke and gave presentations, thanking him for the way God had changed their lives and congregations through his service as their pastor. During this program, God suddenly gave me a passion to be a pastor like Steve—someone whom God could use to lead and influence His Church.

The next day when Maria and I went out for dinner, I asked her if we should be open to leaving Calvary so that I could become a senior pastor. Once again, she nearly fainted from shock! We figured we would be safe for a while, because no church would call a youth and family guy to be their senior pastor. I spent time talking with mentors and creating a profile for the type of church that my gift set would best match. Maria and I remained in denial, thinking that my becoming a senior pastor would be down the road at least a few years.

We occasionally did a little searching on the Willow Creek Association's website to see if any churches with senior pastor openings fit my very narrow profile. One day, I came home from work and Maria said that she had found a church that was "very interesting" in the way it seemingly fit.

"Where is it?" I asked.

"Ventura, California."

I wasn't expecting her to drop that bomb on me! I realize that for most people, the idea of leaving the cold of Minneapolis to head to the warm and sunny climate of Ventura, California, would seem like a no-brainer. But this was completely outside anything we had ever imagined. We're both Mid-westerners, and our entire family lives in Minnesota, Iowa and Illinois. The idea of leaving behind everyone and everything we knew was terrifying.

As I filled out the application and sent my résumé, I figured we would never hear back from them. Yet even though the church received more than 125 applications for the position, somehow—in a way only God can work—my résumé rose to the surface. God was undeniably at work, and in the fall of 2002, I left what I thought was my dream position at Calvary to become the senior pastor of Ventura Missionary Church (VMC).

For seven years, I had the opportunity to take the passion and vision for seeing faith lived out at home into a senior pastor position. I'm incredibly thankful that God brought me to VMC, because I couldn't ask for a more patient, caring, and committed body to serve. Through my time there, God gave me a greater appreciation and understanding for the struggles senior pastors face as they faithfully try to lead their congregations where God wants them to lead.

God Thing #6: A Faith@Home Movement

When I became senior pastor at VMC, I figured I would be leaving my youth and family calling to put on a new hat. Of course, I would bring my passion and commitment to be a Faith@Home church to VMC, because it was one of the reasons they called me. Yet I presumed I'd no longer be helping other churches make Faith@Home a top priority. Little did I know that God had another plan in place.

Shortly after I arrived at VMC, I gave a sermon titled "Home as Church Too." I used the text of Deuteronomy 6 and quoted some statistics from George Barna that supported my message. After one of the services, a member of the church approached me. "Pastor Mark, I really appreciated your message," he said. "The statistics you shared from George Barna were very revealing. Did you know that he lives in Ventura? He occasionally attends VMC, and his daughter is enrolled in our school."

My jaw almost hit the floor! George Barna was a nationally and internationally recognized bestselling author of more than 35 books and the director of The Barna Group, a market research company that specializes in research for Christian ministries. For years, I had been using the research of The Barna Group. George had even once interviewed me over the phone as a part of the research he did for *Transforming Children into Spiritual Champions*, yet we'd never met. The next thing I knew, I was having lunch with him, and we started getting together every month or so just to share ideas with each other.

After I had been at VMC for a little more than a year, George encouraged me at one of our meetings to write a book for parents that would inspire, motivate and equip them to bring Christ and Christlike living into their homes. While I appreciated his encouragement, I had no clue where to start.

Then George said, "Did you know that Gospel Light is located in Ventura and that Bill and Ronnie Greig, who lead Gospel Light, have three children in your school? Tell them I'll write the foreword, and see what they say." Interestingly, Maria and I were coaching a sixth-grade girls' basketball team at our school and the Greigs' daughter was on our team! To make a long story short, Gospel Light published *Faith Begins at Home* and this book, as well as a guide that provides resources to help churches launch faith at home movements in their congregations.

God, in a way that only He can work, had brought together a pastor whom He had instilled with a personal passion and vision, along with one of the nation's leading Christian researchers, and a publishing house to create a movement that would inspire, motivate and equip parents, pastors and church leaders to bring faith back into the home. However, something was still missing: a way to share this vision with pastors.

God Thing #7: A Faith@Home Broadcast Center

While I was writing my first book, I received a phone call from the Willow Creek Association asking me to be a keynote speaker at two upcoming conferences in Canada. Although I had attended numerous Willow Creek conferences, I had never been asked to be a keynote speaker. In fact, I was always blown away by the caliber of their speakers. Every time I heard Bill Hybels deliver his "The Local Church Is the Hope of the World" keynote address, I always walked away thinking I could conquer the world!

The caller from the Willow Creek Association said, "The first conference we would like you to speak at is the Promiseland Conference." The conference at least fit within my comfort zone, because most of the 1,000-plus attendees would be children's ministry pastors. I was used to talking in front of this kind of audience, and children's pastors generally were very warm, encouraging and accepting.

Then the Willow Creek representative dropped a bomb: "We would also like you to be a keynote speaker at the Acts 2 conference following Bill Hybels and Andy Stanley," she said. After I picked myself up off the floor, I realized that God was up to something greater than anything I had ever dreamed of! I now had an opportunity to share the passion and conceptual model that God had given me—and encourage more than 500 senior pastors and leaders to launch Faith@Home movements in their congregations.

Obviously, with all of my two-and-a-half years of senior pastor experience, I felt incredibly nervous and completely in over my head. I surrendered myself and the talk to God, went on stage, and gave it all I had. In yet another sign that God was clearly up to something, when evaluations about the conferences came in a few months later, the talks I gave on making Faith@Home a church's top priority were the highest rated. Now, I know that I'm not nearly the public communicator that Bill Hybels or Andy Stanley is, so it was clear that the Faith@Home message, vision and conceptual model resonated with church leaders. Since then, the Willow Creek Association, along with Focus on the Family (both in Canada and the United States), have committed to helping launch this movement by serving as a broadcast center through the conferences they offer all around the world.

God Thing #8: A Missionary to the Faith@Home Movement
In the spring of 2009, after a significant time of prayer and discernment, I realized that God was calling me to serve the Faith@Home movement full time. I simply couldn't fulfill both the needs of my church and the Faith@Home movement, so I

trusted God and surrendered my position as the senior pastor of VMC to begin a new journey as a missionary to the Faith@Home movement. As a missionary, I now have the privilege of serving as a voice, coach and conduit for this movement that continues to expand across the world.

What Does This All Mean?

Why have I spent so much time taking you through my personal journey? Because I want you to see that the Faith@Home movement is about God and what He has done to give me the passion I have for families. At one point, I didn't own or use a set of Faith@Home lenses. But God changed me and put Faith@Home on my radar as a pastor. I still don't consider myself to be an expert; instead, I would describe myself as a practitioner who is personally invested in helping churches establish and equip homes to be the center of Christlike living. I firmly believe that home is the primary place where faith is nurtured and that parents should be the primary nurturers of faith.

As a result of my own experiences, I now recognize that the majority of today's families have no idea how to make their home a place for nurturing the faith of their children. Therefore, I want to come alongside them and help equip them to bring the love of Jesus Christ into the center of their homes and family life. I believe that only this will lead to families being healthy and strong. As a result, churches will be healthy and strong as well.

I firmly believe that God is at work leading a faith at home movement and that He will lead this movement in and through pastors who are called to serve His Church. I think God is growing tired of the hold Satan has had on families and that He is beginning to awaken pastors to this reality because He desires to reclaim every home. Having people attend church and "play" Christian for two hours on Sunday morning isn't good enough for God. He wants to be a part of our everyday lives. He's not going to rest—and neither should we—until He is a permanent part of our lives at home, work and play!

God changed me. He helped me to see things from a new perspective—the home—that I had completely overlooked. Maybe this is a perspective God wants to give you as well. May the Lord bless you as you prayerfully consider this new perspective.

Let's Get Personal

I'll never forget the time when I spoke at a conference in Switzerland. I had just finished my first keynote presentation, and as I was being taken to lunch, the organizer of the event said, "Now is your lunch session with the senior pastors." I didn't know I had a lunch session with the senior pastors, so I had absolutely nothing prepared.

When I was led into a room that had at least 75 senior pastors in it, I had no idea what I was going to do. Thankfully, the Lord went before me. All I remember was that I felt very vulnerable, so I simply began by sharing a reality that I faced: "Am I the only one who struggles with living out faith at home in my household? I don't know about you, but for me I find that by the time I get home, I'm prayed out, faith talked out, Bibled out, and I have next to nothing to give to my own wife and child. Is that just me or do any of you struggle with that as well?"

What happened next was an outpouring of tears, confession and honest dialogue as we discussed the reality that living out our faith at home is difficult for us as pastors. Many shared that they weren't sure they could lead the Faith@Home movement in their churches, not because they didn't believe it was the right thing to do, but because they knew they weren't doing it themselves and they didn't want to be seen as hypocrites. As I've talked with pastors about making Faith@Home the priority in their churches, I've learned that one thing that keeps many pastors from being passionate about this movement is the struggle of making faith the priority in their own homes. They feel guilty, and they wonder how they can lead something they aren't doing themselves.

I don't want you to be driven by guilt, but read these words from Deuteronomy 6: "Hear, O Israel: The Lord our God, the Lord is one. Love the Lord your God with all your heart and with all your soul and with all your strength. These commandments that I give you today are to be upon your hearts. Impress them on your children" (Deut. 6:4-7). I want to point out what comes immediately before "impress them on your children." The passage reads, "These commandments are to be upon *your* hearts." Similarly, Joshua 24:15 says "as for me" before it says "and my household, we will serve the Lord." Scripture is clear: We can't pass on or infect our churches with something that we don't have ourselves.

The whole movement to bring Christ and Christlike living back into the center of our homes is about *you* and *your* passion and commitment. The Faith@Home movement is less about our churches and more about us. I wish I could say that the statistics regarding faith behavior at home are better for pastors' households than for everyone else, but that simply isn't the case. All I can say is that for me, the Faith@Home movement has made me a better husband and father as well as a better pastor. What matters most to me, though, is my relationship with my wife and daughter. The church was there before me, and it will be there long after I'm gone. I have been called to be an example in faith, life and speech to my wife and daughter first, and then to my church. The same is true for you: What happens in your home is more important than anything you do at church.

When I was preparing to give my Faith@Home message at the Acts 2 conference, where I would be following Bill Hybels and Andy Stanley, I was sitting in the auditorium, getting more and more anxious as Bill and Andy gave incredible, passionate keynote talks (couldn't they deliver a bad message just once!). In between sessions a guy approached me and handed me an envelope that had the following note inside:

Pastor Mark, thank you for coming to Canada and sharing your vision and passion for family ministry with us. After hearing you at the Promiseland conference six weeks ago, I went home and started applying some of the things you shared with us in our own home. I know you were challenging us to lead a Faith@Home movement in our churches, but I realized that I needed to begin that movement in my own home first. You see, I've been a pastor for over 15 years and I have a wife and two children, yet we have never prayed together as a family or read the Bible or done devotions. I went home and began blessing my children, and before I came to this conference they blessed me! Thank you for being a voice that God used to change my life and my ministry.

This note gave me all the encouragement I needed to deliver the message God had called me to deliver.

A Preferred Future

So, whether the Faith@Home message is for you personally or for your church, in either case it will lead to a preferred future. Imagine what could happen to your church if parts of the church body—men's ministry, women's ministry, adult ministry, children's ministry, youth ministry, small-group ministry, senior adult ministry, and so on—all came alongside one another to help bring Christ and Christlike living into its members' homes. If this were to take place, I believe that many of the problems we face as church leaders would go away.

May the Lord bless you as you faithfully provide leadership in your church that will help bring Christ back into the center of your family and every family in your church.

Ponder, Pray and Discuss

1. Did you have a faith-filled home growing up? Did you have parents who set an example of Christlike living for you? Did you pray as a family? Did you attend church and participate in church programs together? Did your parents talk with you about faith or give you a Bible? If you experienced any of these things, take a moment to thank God for your upbringing. You might want to send a thank-you note to your parents, because what you've experienced isn't normal.

2. What about your home life now? Would an outsider describe it as a faith-filled home? How would your children describe it? As a parent, do you try to set an example of Christlike living for your children? Do you pray as a family? Do you talk with your children about faith? Of course, you're a busy pastor and you're at church a lot, but do you ever serve in a ministry together as a family?

3. As you reflect on your family's faith life growing up and your own family's faith life now, how do these experiences affect your view of Faith@Home in the church?

4. If you could take one small step today to bring Christ back into the center of your own family, what would it be? What's stopping you from taking that step?

CHAPTER SUMMARY

- How churches can equip the home to be the main place where faith is nurtured.

- How existing ministry structures in your church can equip families for building faith at home.

- Contemporary calls for making Faith@Home a top priority in the Church.

- Tangible steps to take to become a Faith@Home pastor and church.

- The weakness of "add a silo" family ministry.

- The strength of being a church of Faith@Home.

- Why Faith@Home means donning a new set of lenses.

- How Take It Home events inspire, provide practice for faith skills and equip families to take home the skills.

- How a meaningful series of Take It Home events can become a string weaving together all that your church does.

- The cumulative and transformational effects of Take It Home events.

- Ways to extend the Faith@Home vision beyond children, youth and family ministry.

- The fun of tweaking what you already do in your own church.

- This is revolutionarily simple. You can do it!

3

What Should We Do About It?

One of the most serious tasks of the church at large is to help its member families to be the body of Christ within the home—to become settings where unconditional love, affirmation, challenge to accountability, and forgiveness are known; to learn and share rituals, symbols, and stories of faith; to recognize and claim their special gifts and mission in the world [1]
MARJORIE THOMPSON

ANOTHER VOICE SAYS...

Melinda Kinsman, Beaverton Foursquare Church
Portland, Oregon

Two weekends ago, we had our third-grade Take It Home event. It was focused on communion. We served the ceremonial portion of the Passover Seder as part of the event, in addition to explaining the meaning of communion. It was a great event, made better by an unusual encounter.

The evening of the event, I was in church and was approached by a woman in her late 20s or early 30s who shared that she had been in attendance at the Take It Home event on Sunday morning. The situation is that she is single (never been married), is a leader in our junior-high ministry and lives with another single woman who is pre-Christian, not interested in church and has two children—boys, one a third-grader and the other a sixth-grader. The boys expressed an interest in attending church with her, so on the

Sunday of the Take It Home event, she brought them to church for the first time. The sixth-grader attended his age-level ministry, and she joined the third-grader in the gym for the Take It Home event. So the picture here is a single woman sitting in the event with a boy who is not her son and who has never been to church.

She shared with me that the third-grader loved the Seder, enjoying the "dare" of eating parsley and horseradish. That afternoon, both boys pelted her with question after question about God, with the end result being that both boys made a decision to receive Jesus that afternoon! Yea, God!

I know at times a concern is voiced: "What about the kids who don't have parents in the home who will do this with them?" Here is an example of the diverse nature of families in our culture and one person stepping up to be family in a big way to these two boys. This is one example that faith at home does work for all manner, shape and size of homes! The nature of our direct ministry to kids has not changed—except, I hope, to become more effective—but by including Faith@Home Take It Home events, we are reaching families in a very practical hands-on way and in surprising evangelistic ways. God is good!

Let's pause a minute to recap. We've determined that God is calling the Church to rise up and address the area that Satan is attacking the most: our homes. At the same time, we've learned that parents today want to have a better family than the one they grew up in. And we've concluded that it's time for the Church to come alongside households and equip them to bring Christ into the center of their homes.

If that's where we are, what's next? We now face the challenge—and the opportunity—of determining how we can equip the home to be the primary place where faith is nurtured and how that equipping can take place through our existing ministry structures.

When I was growing up, my dad would often repeat an expression that you've probably heard: "You can either be part of the problem or part of the solution." These words certainly apply as we face the reality that Christlike living isn't happening in our homes today in spite of some of the best programs the Church has ever offered. As church leaders, we can either be part of the problem or part of the solution. In other words, we can either continue enabling this to happen or we can do something about it.

In the last chapter, I told you about my personal journey that led me to surrender myself to serve this Faith@Home movement full time. When I learned that parents are two to three times more influential in passing on faith to their children than any church program, I knew that I had to make some changes. At that point in my ministry, I was spending 99.9 percent of my time focusing on things that were happening at the church. Of course, this left little or no time to focus on helping equip homes to be the primary place where faith is nurtured.

Like a lot of pastors, I used to define success as more people coming to more activities at the church so that we could build more buildings that would enable us to offer more events for more people at church! Whew—what a rat race! To be honest, I wasn't even aware that I needed to be concerned with what was taking place in homes. I had no idea that less than 10 percent of the people in my church were praying, reading the Bible or doing devotions in their homes.[2] I had no idea that the majority of parents had abdicated their faith-nurturing responsibilities to us, the "experts," through our programs.

Yet the glassy stares I received on Sunday mornings as I made suggestions for what parents could do in their weekly devotions should have told me all I needed to know. When I witnessed what was happening in families at our church on a weekly basis and watched the divorce rate among Christian couples in America climb as high or even a little higher than the overall divorce rate, I shouldn't have been surprised that these types of things weren't taking place in the home.[3]

A Biblical Mandate

When I speak to pastors about this issue, I find that they're usually not shocked by the information about the condition of families.

The situation might be a bit worse than they originally thought, but they still aren't too surprised. A person doesn't have to be in ministry very long to realize that Christlike living isn't happening in homes today.

It also doesn't take a lot of convincing for church leaders to realize that parents are far more influential than church programs. And most pastors realize, as the following passages clearly show, that God intends and calls us to equip people to live out faith at home:

- For I have chosen [Abraham], so that he will direct his children and his household after him to keep the way of the Lord (Gen. 18:19).

- Train a child in the way he should go, and when he is old he will not turn from it (Prov. 22:6).

- These commandments that I give you today are to be upon your hearts. Impress them on your children. Talk about them when you sit at home and when you walk along the road, when you lie down and when you get up. Tie them as symbols on your hands and bind them on your foreheads. Write them on the doorframes of your houses and on your gates (Deut. 6:6-9).

- But if serving the Lord seems undesirable to you, then choose for yourselves this day whom you will serve, whether the gods your forefathers served beyond the River, or the gods of the Amorites, in whose land you are living. But as for me and my household, we will serve the Lord (Josh. 24:15).

- He decreed statutes for Jacob and established the law in Israel, which he commanded our forefathers to teach their children, so the next generation would know them, even the children yet to be born, and they in turn would tell their children. Then they would put their trust in God and would not forget his deeds but would keep his commands (Ps. 78:5-8).

- Children, obey your parents in the Lord, for this is right. "Honor your father and mother"—which is the first commandment with a promise—"that it may go well with you and that you may enjoy long life on the earth." Fathers, do not exasperate your children; instead, bring them up in the training and instruction of the Lord (Eph. 6:1-4).

Other Voices

The Faith@Home crisis is a reality. Take a look at just a few of the many leaders who are emphasizing the need for faith at home to be a top priority in the church:

- *TomSchultz, Group Publishing:* "If you're not doing family ministry, you're not doing youth ministry." This quote appeared on the cover of a 1995 issue of *Group* magazine. At the time, Group Publishing had very few family ministry resources. Since then, the company has woven family ministry and Faith@Home components into much of their materials and resources.

- *Larry Fowler, Director of AWANA Clubs International:* "Research consistently affirms the declining biblical worldview (a perspective of life grounded in biblical truth) of our young people. It is nothing short of a crisis, even among committed Christian families! What will stop it? There is very little anyone can do, unless the home (and hence the parents) are involved at the core."[4] For many years, AWANA Clubs International was an effective yet church-based children's ministry program. AWANA has made a significant change in their methodology to become more Faith@Home intentional through their AWANA clubs.

• *Roland Martinson, Luther Seminary:* "The church's role is
to be equippers of families. What we ought to do is let
the kids drop their parents off at church, train the parents and send them back to their mission field, their
home, to grow Christians." Dr. Martinson has boldly led
the way in developing a seminary training program for
pastors that focuses on Faith@Home.

• *Marjorie Thompson, Director of Pathways Center for Christian
Spirituality:* "The family, more than any other context of
life, is the foundational place of spiritual formation in
its broad sense, especially for children. If the church
wishes to see the content of this formation as explicitly
Christian, it will need to take the role and support of
the family far more seriously than it has."[5] Marjorie
Thompson, an ordained minister in the Presbyterian
Church (USA), has a long-standing interest in the area
of spiritual formation. Her book *The Family as Forming
Center* was originally published in 1996 in response to a
consultation on family spirituality sponsored by The
Upper Room. The consultation was both timely and
ahead of its time, as the level of interest in the role of
families has risen dramatically since then—both in church
and in culture.

• *Christian Smith and Melinda Denton, Sociologists of Religion:*
"In sum, therefore, we think that the best general rule of
thumb that parents might use to reckon their children's
most likely religious outcomes is this: 'We'll get what we
are.' By normal processes of socialization, and unless
other significant forces intervene, more than what parents might say they want as religious outcomes in their
children, most parents most likely will end up getting re-
ligiously of their children what they themselves are."[6]
Smith and Denton's book *Soul Searching* offers one of the
most comprehensive studies on the religious and spiri-

tual lives of American teenagers and clearly identifies the critical need for Faith@Home.

In fact, these contemporary calls for making Faith@Home a top priority in the Church simply echo what preacher, theologian and missionary Jonathan Edwards realized in the American colonial era: "Every Christian family ought to be as if it were a little church consecrated to Christ, and wholly influenced and governed by his rule."[7]

Getting Practical

As I travel and speak, I spend less time trying to convince pastors and church leaders that a Faith@Home problem exists. Instead, I find myself focusing the majority of my time on what we can do about it. That's what we're going to do now—provide some tangible steps that you can take to become a Faith@Home-focused pastor and church.

Right Way and Wrong Way

Over the past 15 to 20 years, as churches have become more aware of the need for Faith@Home, I've witnessed the emergence of two family models or methodologies. The first is what I will call the add-a-silo family ministry model. In this model, the church approaches family ministry the same way we approach everything else—through programs. The infants and toddlers go into the nursery program, the three-year-olds through sixth-graders go through the Sunday School program, the junior-highers and senior-highers end up in the youth ministry program, and the adults get placed in the adult Sunday school or into another small-group ministry. Each silo develops a program approach to grow and pass on the faith to those within its ministry.

So, when a church wakes up to the reality that it needs to focus on Faith@Home, it takes the same approach and simply adds a silo (program) called "family ministry." The church creates a family ministry team that organizes family game nights, family camps, family retreats, family date nights, and many other creative family programs.

Unfortunately, I have found that even with the best intentions and efforts, these family ministry programs typically result in a turnout of only 4 out of 10 families. I know this is the case because I've tried family ministry programs this way myself! Even when we offered an event with the nation's best speakers and I used every promotional tool available, only about 40 percent of our families would attend. And most of those who attended were already passing on the faith in their homes and didn't need the help! We were trying to add another activity to an already-too-busy calendar of events and weren't reaching the parents and families who truly needed to be trained and equipped to bring Christ into the center of their homes.

Add a Silo

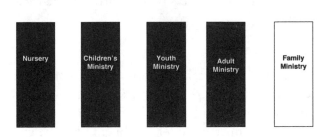

While the add-a-silo model is clearly the most predominant model for family ministry—because it represents what we know how to do—it isn't the most effective. If we want to bring true transformation to more families, we must embrace a comprehensive and integrated approach to Faith@Home and become Faith@Home-focused churches.

A Faith@Home-Focused Church

For the last 25 years or so, the Church has gone through a significant discipleship transformation as a result of the small-group ministry movement. How effective this movement has been in individual churches seems to be connected to the approach each church takes to small-group ministry.

Maybe you've heard the catchphrase attached to the small-group movement: "You can be a church *with* small groups or you can be a church *of* small groups." Interestingly, this is just another way of saying that you can take a program approach to small-group ministry by adding a separate small-group program to everything else and produce a marginal impact, or you can make small groups an integrated part of how you do ministry as a church and exponentially increase the effectiveness of the transformation in people's lives.

In the same way, you can be a church *with* a family ministry—the add-a-silo model—and have marginal impact. Or you can become a Faith@Home-focused church. In this model, you learn to look at everything that the church does through lenses of bringing faith and Christlike living back into the center of every household.

A Faith@Home-Focused Church

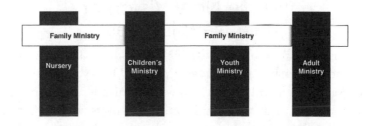

In a Faith@Home-focused church, instead of adding a family ministry silo or adding family ministry to the children's ministry director's job description, the goal of every ministry of the church is to equip the home to be the primary place where faith is nurtured. In a Faith@Home-focused church, you appropriately elevate Faith@Home to be a part of how you do church. It looks something like this:

- Your men's and women's ministries equip men and women to live out their faith at home.
- Your small-group ministry focuses on equipping people and holds them accountable for living out their faith in their homes.
- Your prayer ministry equips every family to pray daily in their homes instead of focusing on a few big prayer events at the church.
- Each sermon you preach will include an emphasis on taking the message home and living it out daily.
- Every Bible study your church does equips adults to be like Christ in their homes, community and world.
- Your children's ministry helps equip parents to engage in faith skills with their children at home.
- Your youth ministry helps parents get engaged (or stay engaged) with their teenagers' faith journey at home.

Notice that these ministries focus on what is happening in the *home*, not what is happening at *church*.

Whole New Vision or Just New Lenses?

Another way of looking at Faith@Home is not to think of it as a whole new vision but as a new set of lenses. Once your church puts on these lenses, it will begin to view its ministries in a completely different way. This new way of looking at things will dramatically impact the vision of your church.

Please hear me when I say that the last thing your church needs to fix the Faith@Home problem is a whole new program. There is no new program out there that will fix the Faith@Home problem. Rather, this problem can only be corrected when your church takes active steps to correct its "eyesight" problem that has been preventing it from fully making its vision come into focus. I believe that God provides each church with a clear vision. Your church might not need to change its vision or strategy, but in order to be the church God wants you to be, you might need to put on the Faith@Home lenses so that your church can clearly see that vision become a reality.

Satan knows just how strong the Church can be when its members gather together around a common vision. It's like grabbing a handful of pencils and trying to break them all at once—not very easy to do. However, if Satan can divide the families in the Church, it becomes more like breaking a single pencil—which is a lot easier for him to do. So Satan keeps churches from achieving their vision by breaking families and getting faith out of the home.

Therefore, without your Faith@Home lenses on, your church's vision for the elderly woman or the college-age student can't be fully realized. The home is the place where your vision as a church will be carried out. We've mistakenly thought that the church vision gets carried out at church, but it doesn't.

Back to the Future

If you think about it, the Faith@Home vision shouldn't be difficult for us to embrace. It's the way the church used to operate. The catechism was developed as an instructional tool for parents to pass on the basic teachings of the Church to their children. George Barna describes it in *Revolution*:

Christian families taught the ways of God in their homes every day. Parents were expected to model a Spirit-led lifestyle for their children, and families were to make their home a sanctuary for God. In a very real sense, the home was the early church—supplemented by larger gatherings in the Temple and elsewhere, but never replaced by what took place in the homes of believers.[8]

In some ways, therefore, we need to return to the way things used to be in order to reestablish the home as the primary place where faith is nurtured. As I stated earlier, I don't think the Church needs to get rid of Sunday School, youth ministry, men's ministry and other programs. Instead, we need to rethink and change our approach to how to do these ministries. What do existing ministries like nursery, Sunday School, youth ministry, small-group ministry and others look like in a Faith@Home-focused church? Let's take a look.

Faith@Home-focused Nursery

The first ministry silo in most churches is the nursery ministry. Many churches have a nursery room staffed with nursery volunteers who create a safe environment where parents feel comfortable leaving their infants. This nursery ministry is usually used for the first three years of a child's life, and it is probably considered by most parents to be a drop-off haven, a safe place to leave their child for a while. But is that all we want this ministry to be? Shouldn't we be using these early childhood years to establish a partnership with the parents? And, actually, shouldn't the partnership start when parents first bring their newborn to us?

What is the first thing that parents usually ask the church to do for them when they have a newborn child? That's right: dedication or baptism, depending on your church's tradition. So what do we pastors do? We figure out a mutually agreed upon date when we will effectively "do their child." When the big day comes, we bring the parents and the baby forward in church, we hold the baby, we dedicate or baptize the baby, we hand the baby back to the parents, everyone applauds, and we send the parents home with the baby. We even keep statistics about how many babies we dedicate or baptize a year! How is this Faith@Home focused? Let me share another way to do this.

Whenever parents have called up my church and asked us to dedicate or baptize their child, we have simply said that we would love to but that we need to meet with them first to discuss it. When the parents and I have met, I've always begun by simply asking them one question: "Why do you want to have your child dedicated or baptized?" Unprepared for this question, they've usually responded with the answer that is always the right answer: "Jesus!" I've then pressed them a little further and asked, "Why Jesus? What is it about Jesus that is so important to you?" Eventually they share that they want their child to know and follow Christ so that he [or she] will enjoy all that God has planned for their child, including eternal life.

I've agreed that this intention is certainly a good one, and then I've asked them what type of faith they would like their child to have: "Do you want your child to have a faith that is one-hour-at-church-only, a faith that your child will one day walk away from altogether, or do you want your child to have an authentic faith that sticks with him [or her] for life?" They have chosen the latter, the obvious choice; and then I have said, "Would you like an 80-percent chance that your child will have an authentic faith that lasts, or would you prefer a 26-percent chance?" Once again the choice has been obvious, and then I've revealed to them the statistics found in the "Most Significant Religious Influences" survey, in particular the results that prove that parents are two or three times more influential on their children than any church program (see the chart on page 29). I have emphasized the fact that *they* will be the determining factor on whether or not their child will have a lifelong faith.

At this point the parents have usually begun to get uncomfortable, so I've simply said, "At this point, it probably seems like I'm dumping a huge responsibility on you that you probably don't know how to fulfill. I was wondering if you would like a little help in doing this, because we would love to be your lifelong partner that will show you how to pass on the faith to your child." I've then told them that the purpose of dedication or baptism is to do exactly what they needed: The parents *and* the church will be committing themselves to raising this child to know, love and follow Christ.

A baptism at our church is fairly straightforward. (The following baptism model can, of course, be easily adapted for a dedication service.) We first ask the parents if they will commit themselves to be the primary examples of faith for their child by loving the Lord with all of their heart, soul and strength. Then we ask the grandparents and/or godparents to step up as lifelong spiritual mentors for these parents—to help, encourage and equip them to be Faith@Home-focused parents. Finally, we turn to the congregation and ask them to commit to being the extended family of God for these parents, to help them be Faith@Home-focused parents by providing a men's, women's, children's and youth ministry that will equip them to fulfill their responsibilities. After these commitments are made, we then baptize the child in the name of the Father, Son and Holy Spirit.

Following the baptism, we present the family a Faith Chest, which is a small wooden hope chest made by the men of our church.[9] We explain that this Faith Chest is something that over the course of the child's life we, the church along with the grandparents and/or godparents, will fill with resources that will help the parents teach their child about Christ and His ways.

On the anniversary of the baptism, our women's ministry (they were jealous of all the attention the men were getting for the faith chests) delivers a gift to the family for the Faith Chest in order to remind them of the commitment we made to them and the commitment they made to their child. This partnership causes the parents to look at the nursery ministry—and the church as a whole—as much more than just a safe drop-off place. As you can see, we used these first three years to establish the Faith@Home partnership.

Wouldn't you like to have a dedication or baptism that is a little more like this faith-at-home focused baptism?

Instilling Faith@Home Through Sunday School

One of the greatest challenges we faced in the church where I pastored was getting parents to show up for Faith@Home training and equipping events. What if I told you that we discovered how to get a 98 percent turnout rate for events that equip parents to pass on the faith themselves? Would that pique your interest? Well that's exactly what we were able to do. Here's how we did it.

We began by asking ourselves, what faith skills should every family be equipped to practice in the home? In other words, what does an "as for me and my household we will serve the Lord" family look like? Before long, we had a healthy list of activities and disciplines, such as prayer, Bible reading, devotions, blessings, family service projects, and so on.

After we compiled the list, we determined at what age each faith skill should be taught in the home so that it can be firmly established. For example, it probably wouldn't be a good idea for parents to wait until their children are teenagers before they start the ritual of blessing them. However, if parents start the ritual of blessing before a child turns five, it can become an established practice that continues through the teenage years and beyond.

Armed with our list of faith skills and predetermined ages for when each skill should be established, we then put together a Faith@Home training and equipping workshop for each specific faith skill. We called our family training and equipping workshops "Take It Home" events. Instead of scheduling them for an additional time that families would need to come to church, we built them into our Sunday School and youth ministry programs. This made it much easier for parents to participate in the events, because they occurred at a time when they were already bringing their children to church.

At least once a year, we would require parents to attend Sunday School with their children. On that day, they would learn a new faith skill that they could immediately implement in their home. Over time, families began to anticipate upcoming Take It Home events because they knew they would receive training to help them as a family. (In a different church I served, we held 22 Take It Home events a year. This meant that some parents had to come to two events per year, which they were glad to do because these events made them better families of faith.)

On the following page is an example of how a series of Take It Home events could play out during a child's years at home. Remember that these events take place on different Sundays throughout the year.

Take It Home Basics
Take It Home events essentially are the same length of time as your children's ministry program, so in most cases they last one hour.

TARGET AGE	EVENT	WHAT IT TEACHES
Infants	Dedication/Infant Baptism	How Mom and Dad are primary faith influencers and the church is a lifelong partner
2-3	Family Blessings	How to ritually bless your child
3-4	Family Devotions	How to have family devotions
5-6	My Church	How to enjoy going to church
7-8	Prayer	How to pray together
8-9	Family Serve	How to do family service projects
9-10	My Bible	How to read the Bible together
10-11	Worship	How to worship together at home
11-12	Money and Me	How to manage your money
12-13	Computer and Music Boundaries	What is okay to look at/listen to and what is not
13-14	A Second Option	How to establish a Christian mentor
14-16	Dating, Kissing, Sex and Stuff	That true love waits
17-18	Looking into the Future	Spiritual gifts and following God

During the Take It Home event, four things around the faith skill are focused on:

1. Parents are *motivated* to want to do the faith skill in the home. In most cases, we use the testimony of a family who had been transformed by bringing the faith skill into their everyday life at home. What we discovered is that when parents are properly motivated, they will try just about anything!

2. The faith skill is *modeled*, and parents learn how to do the skill in the home. In most cases we showcase multiple ways to practice whichever faith skill we're highlighting—whether it's prayer, reading the Bible, worshiping,

blessing, and so on—so that families can see how easily the skill can be incorporated into their lifestyle.

3. The families *practice* the faith skill, because the hardest time is always the first time. We realized that if we could help them have a successful first experience, there was a much greater likelihood that they would continue to use the skill in the home.

4. We *provide* families with a resource that will give them what they need to continue engaging in the faith skill at home. Providing a free resource to take home shows the church's commitment to equipping families to do the skill themselves at home.

Other Take It Home Events

The *Take It Home* implementation guide that I co-authored with Dave Teixeira provides complete outlines for 14 Take It Home events that you can customize for your church.[10] Let me share a few examples of Take It Home events so that you can better understand how they help bring the Faith@Home vision into your church's ministry.

Prayer (for Parents of Four- and Five-Year-Olds)

As families arrived, they sat at round tables, and we began with a skit or DVD focusing on prayer. We showed our favorite movie scene about prayer, the painful prayer by Whoopi Goldberg's character in the movie *Sister Act,* where she is asked to pray and clearly has no idea what to say. We quickly pointed out to the families that no matter how bad they may be at prayer, they won't be as bad as Whoopi Goldberg's character!

Then, to motivate the families, we introduced them to a church family who also had once lacked this skill, the Thompson family: Michael (the dad), Theresa (the mother) and Trevor (their eight-year-old son). Theresa shared the story of how she had coerced Michael into attending this same Take It Home event four years earlier by telling him that this was the only thing she wanted for her anniversary. Michael recalled, "I figured this was a lot cheaper than a trip to Cancun, so I figured what the heck."

They went on to explain that prior to this event, they had never prayed with their son, Trevor, but now prayer has become a huge part of their family. Michael went on to share that Trevor would not go to sleep until he had prayed with his dad, and Michael stated that his prayer time with Trevor was the best time of his day. They then concluded their testimony by singing (yes, singing!) their favorite mealtime prayer, which was the Superman prayer![11] When they were done, we had a bunch of motivated parents who were willing to give prayer a shot, because they had seen the impact prayer had made for the Thompsons. (One thing to keep in mind: We intentionally focused our time of motivation toward the dads because we felt that if we could motivate the dads, everyone else in the families would be motivated as well.)

Following the time of motivation, we modeled five ways to do mealtime prayer, nighttime prayer and anytime prayer. Then we had each family pick and practice one of the mealtime, nighttime and anytime prayers. We concluded the event by presenting each household with a copy of *Faith Begins at Home*, a prayer book that provides ideas to keep prayer ongoing in the home.

"My Bible" Take It Home Event
Every year, our church had the same tradition. On a Sunday morning each October, the third-graders marched up to the front of the worship area. The pastor called each child forward and personally presented a Bible to him or her. After all the children received their Bibles, the congregation applauded and the children left the sanctuary.

Don't get me wrong—this was okay. I obviously liked the idea of the church providing a Bible for each third-grader. Yet after I became infected with the faith at home vision, I remember asking a simple question: "How does this help bring Bible reading into the home?"

So the next year, we decided to have a Take It Home event called "My Bible" one week before the Bible presentation Sunday.

Parents accompanied their third-graders to this event. On each table, we placed two or three old Bibles that belonged to some of our senior adults. The pages throughout were written on and various passages were highlighted. Instantly, the kids were drawn to the Bibles and the handwritten notes.

We took some time to teach families about the basics of the Bible, the difference between the Old and New Testaments, and why reading the Word of God is so important. We then gave the kids an opportunity to pick out a new Bible and allowed them to sit down at their tables and make personalized Bible covers. We knew this craft activity would keep most of the kids busy for a while.

As the students worked on their Bible covers, we took the parents to a different room and introduced them to Mr. Reinhardt. Mr. Reinhardt, who's about 70 years old, shared that he received a Bible from his dad when he was in third grade. He explained that inside the front cover of the Bible was a personal note his dad had written him. Before he read the note to the parents, he explained how important it was to him. "About a year after my dad gave me this Bible, he was killed in a farming accident," Mr. Reinhardt said. "My dad was a man of few words, but this note has been the one thing that has kept me close to him all these years." When he read the note his dad had written, many of the parents cried. So did I.

After a few moments of reflection, we asked the parents to write a note in their children's new Bibles. Believe me, they wrote serious notes! The following Sunday, instead of simply marching the kids forward, we invited the parents to come to the front with their third-graders. We presented the Bible to the parents and explained that this was part of the church's role in coming alongside them. In turn, the parents presented the Bibles to their children, and the third-graders opened their Bibles to read for the first time the personal notes written inside. For many of the students, it was the first time they had ever received a personal note from their parents.

Inside the back cover of the Bible, we provided a Bible reading guide that the kids could use to highlight two verses a day during the coming year. We also gave them a challenge: "Maybe one day, your Bible can look like the Bibles you saw last week in your class-room!" You could tell by looking at the eyes of these third-graders that they were up to the challenge! Over the course of the next year, those Bibles were used and highlighted in the homes!

The idea for this event involved taking an event the church was already doing and adding a layer that equipped faith to happen at home. If we want families to read the Bible in their homes, we need to do our part to inspire, motivate and equip them to do it. Through our Take It Home events, which were woven into Sunday School, we were equipping families to pray, bless, read the Bible, worship and serve in the home.

Faith@Home in Youth Ministry

In youth ministry, things get a little trickier because many of the students whom youth pastors will work with come from households that do not engage in Faith@Home activities. Therefore, youth pastors need to have a both-and-and approach to youth ministry.

Both . . .

Youth pastors today need to do whatever they can to reach students for Christ and equip them to be Faith@Home-focused followers of Christ, whether or not their parents or friends are doing it. Youth pastors cannot simply be satisfied with getting students to come to church events; they need to leverage their youth ministry events to equip these students to have a lifelong 24/7 faith.

And . . .

Youth ministers cannot simply give up on parents but need to find ways to engage or reengage parents in the faith journey with their teenagers. This is a scary reality for youth pastors who in many cases are younger than the parents and may not even have children yet. "Who am I to tell parents what to do when I don't have kids myself?" Let me handle that commonly made statement by youth pastors as gently as I can: That's a cop-out! (How was that for soft-pedaling it?)

Youth pastors who want students to have a faith that lasts should be as motivated as anyone to equip parents to be engaged, because although in a few years the youth pastor will no longer be a spiritual influence in these young adults' lives, the parents still will be. Will this be as easy as doing another fund-raiser or retreat? No, but that doesn't give youth pastors an excuse not to do it. A youth pastor simply has to come to grips with the reality that what Mom and Dad do or don't do regarding faith will *always* be much more influential than any retreat or other youth event. Youth pastors must find ways to engage the parents—and it may not be as difficult as you may think.

Dave Teixeira used to serve as my youth and family ministries pastor when I was still senior pastor at VMC. Each year, he led a weekend retreat titled "Dating, Kissing, Sex, and Stuff" for 12- to 14-year-olds. He took the teenagers off to a Bible camp where he taught and challenged them to make wise, biblical decisions as they prepared to enter their dating years. Dave didn't hold back any punches, and the retreat was always very influential and life changing for the teenagers who attended.

Inevitably, though, when the teens returned home from the retreat, they got off the bus, and there were Mom and Dad, anxiously waiting to hear how things had gone. One of the parents would inevitably ask his or her teen, "How was the retreat?"

Even if the retreat had been the most life-changing experience the teen had ever had, the teen's response usually was simply, "It was okay." And that was the end of the communication between parent and teen on this very important subject.

When Dave became infected with the Faith@Home vision, he faced a difficult realization. During all the years he had led the retreat, he had done so in an effort to help parents out by discussing a difficult topic with their teens. However, Dave now realized that by not involving parents, he was robbing them of an experience that could bring them closer together with their teenage sons and daughters. While most youth pastors would have scored this event a success because of the great attendance and the life-changing influence it had on the teens, Dave realized that the retreat, as currently formatted, was a failure. So he made a change to make the retreat an event that equipped parents to impart faith at home.

The next year, Dave brought the parents in two hours before the students returned from the retreat. He went through the teachings he had covered on the retreat and then provided questionnaires that parents could use to start a discussion with their teenagers. When the students arrived, Dave brought them together with their parents and led a final session. With their parents as witnesses, the students made commitments to abstain from sexual activity before marriage! Many parents thanked Dave for helping them have the discussion they knew they needed to have.

And...

The final aspect of a Faith@Home youth ministry is the role youth pastors play in supporting the Faith@Home movement in children's ministry. Youth pastors should be the biggest advocates and supporters of making Take It Home events happen in children's ministry, because what happens in children's ministry greatly impacts youth ministry.

I served a large congregation in a church that had been implementing Take It Home events for over 15 years prior to my arrival. As the youth and family pastor, I was responsible for overseeing the children's and youth ministry programs, and one of the programs that I learned I was to oversee was a teen worship service that happened on Wednesday nights. More than 300 teenagers typically showed up for the youth service, and then following the service, the teens would meet in small groups, which meant that we had to find over 60 adults who would be willing to spend two hours every Wednesday night with squirrelly junior-high students.

Many adults would consider this a nightmare job; but when I sat down with the junior-high youth pastor, I was stunned to learn that not only were no small-group leaders needed but also a waiting list of them existed! I couldn't imagine that this could really be the case, so she showed me the list. I was blown away because the majority of teenagers wanted their parents to serve as their small-group leaders! In fact, we had so many parents who wanted to participate in and attend the Wednesday night service that we had to open our worship-center balcony to accommodate them all. How was this possible? Simple. The church had equipped the parents to nurture faith at home. When their children were age three, the parents had been taught how to bless their kids in the home. When their kids were age four, the parents learned how to pray in the home. When the children were age five, the families learned how to read the Bible together.

If you are a youth pastor, wouldn't you like to inherit teenagers who come from households that pray, read the Bible and worship in the home? If so, then you need to help make this happen by making Take It Home events part of children's ministry. By the time the effects on teens is seen, you may not be the youth pastor at that particular church anymore, but the next youth pastor will thank you for implementing the Faith@Home movement. Start today to use the both-and-and approach to youth ministry. You want to *both* reach students for Christ and equip them to be Faith@Home focused; *and* you want to find a way to engage and equip parents to be a part of the students faith journey; *and* you want to actively support the Faith@Home movement by advocating Take It Home events in children's ministry.

Faith@Home Adult Ministries

How do you weave Faith@Home into adult ministries? Although what I describe below is specifically about a men's ministry, its lesson applies equally well to women's ministry.

When I was serving at Ventura Missionary Church, we had a strong men's ministry that had a monthly men's dinner. The monthly dinner consisted of a great tri-tip steak dinner followed by a time of worship led by our men's worship team, and that was followed by a guest speaker. The men's leadership team was responsible for lining up the guest speakers, and we were always in search of a recognizable person who we could bring in to speak. On one occasion we were able to get the general manager of the

Los Angeles Dodgers, Ned Colletti, to come and speak; and all the guys showed up wearing their LA Dodger jerseys.

A couple of weeks later, I was specifically asked to come to their next meeting. At the meeting, I watched as the chair of our men's ministry went to a whiteboard and said, "Pastor has been talking a lot about faith at home, and I have been wondering how our men's ministry is Faith@Home focused. For example, we had Ned Colletti here, and a lot of guys showed up; but how did that event help them live out their faith at home?" He then drew a stick figure on the whiteboard and asked, "I was wondering, what are some things a Faith@Home man would do? What are some things he wouldn't do?" Everyone started to provide answers: A Faith@Home man would be a man of prayer, integrity, service; and he would not engage in things like pornography, adultery—the men went on to make a pretty long list of positive character traits. Our chairman then simply said, "What if we were to get speakers on these topics instead?"

One of the men in the group knew Sam Gallucci, co-author of the book *Road Warrior: How to Keep Your Faith, Relationships and Integrity Away from Home*, which helps men avoid burnout and temptations when traveling, and we asked him to come and speak to the group. Which do you think was the better men's dinner? The one where a bunch of guys showed up wearing Dodger jerseys or the one where we learned how to abstain from engaging in pornography and other temptations while traveling on the road? We still did the same men's dinners, but they now had a Faith@Home focus.

So, if you want to have a Faith@Home-focused adult ministry, simply ask the following questions:

- What would a Faith@Home-focused man, woman, single and so forth look like?
- What would they do?
- What would they not do?
- Is our ministry equipping these individuals to do and not do these things?
- If not, how could our ministry do a better job?

Faith@Home Seniors' Ministry

The Faith@Home vision is very important for the oldest members of your congregation. Again, I'll use my experience at VMC as an example of how to incorporate the principles of the movement in your ministry for seniors.

Our seniors' ministry got on board by offering its own Take It Home event titled "How to Be a Meddling Grandparent." I was asked to provide the motivational talk, and I began by stating that I had heard from many of the seniors that they wished the Faith@Home focus would have come to them 25 years earlier. "A lot of you have said to me, 'Pastor Mark, where was this Faith@Home message 25 years ago?' Well, all I can say to you is that I don't know. I don't know why it wasn't here 25 years ago, and I know a lot of you feel guilty because you know you didn't practice faith at home; and as a result, many of your kids have walked away from the faith. I realize this is painful for you; but please hear me as I say that the Faith@Home message is here today, and you are still your children's parents. Therefore, it's time to get over your guilt by recognizing that there is grace, and get back in the game! Even if your kids are now in their 30s or 40s, what you say and do is still more influential than anything I can say or do at church. Satan realizes that and he is using guilt to keep you out of the game. But our God is the God of second chances, and you have new life in Christ, so it's time to get back in the game."

Three seniors then each gave an example of how they have stayed in the game with their kids and grandchildren. The first was a woman over 70 years old who shared how she used a cell phone and text messaging to send Scripture verses to her kids and grandkids once a week. "It takes me forever to press these little buttons," she said, "but I have the time." The next speaker was a man who shared how he used Internet sites to send inspirational and motivational stories to his kids. The last senior to speak was a woman who said, "I don't have a cell phone or computer, so I hope this is okay; but all I do is write my grandchildren a letter once a week." How many of us would love to get such a letter once a week?

The seniors were then asked to write a letter to their kids and/or grandkids (a stack of blank paper had been put on each table before the seniors met). It was acknowledged that for some, the letter might need to be an apology for simply taking their kids to church but never engaging in any faith talk with them at home. (We later heard from many of these seniors that the letter they wrote led their kids to give God another chance!)

I firmly believe that we need to have Faith@Home-focused seniors who are empowered and released to meddle in the spiritual lives of their children and grandchildren. There is no retirement plan when it comes to passing on the faith! In fact, I tell seniors who seem timid or even afraid to be a spiritual influence in their children's or grandchildren's lives that they can stop only when Satan stops. When Satan stops trying to lead their children and grandchildren away from God, then they can stop trying to lead them to follow God.

Faith@Home Worship

I'll never forget when my postmodern worship leader asked me at one of our worship planning meetings, "Pastor Mark, could you tell me how our worship is Faith@Home focused?" At first I was offended and I thought to myself, *How dare he ask me that question. I'm Mister Faith@Home!* But he simply went on to explain that he was wrestling with why the Sunday service needed to end at church. This discussion eventually led us to develop Take It Homework, which the church now provides each Sunday in the bulletin. The homework enables people to look up additional Scriptures based on the message of that day and to continue discussion about and application of the message at home that week. This simple change ensures that even our worship service has a Faith@Home focus!

A Critical String

I hope these examples have helped provide a picture of what things can look like for a Faith@Home-focused church. As you can now see, this is not a family ministry program, but it is a way of doing church. Establishing some sort of Take It Home strategy—whether you call it that or not—that weaves through all your ministries is a critical step in becoming a Faith@Home-focused church. The Take It Home events can become a string that weaves through and holds together all you do with children, youth and adults. Without this string, it's easy for each ministry (silo) to run in its own direction. This leads to your church becoming program driven with a congregation spread a mile wide but with faith only an inch deep.

Too Simple?

I know that you might be thinking that this all seems too easy. How could one event per year lead to significant change? My response is simply that you are right; one event a year *won't* lead to significant change at home. But these aren't one-time-only events. They are training and equipping experiences!

None of the Take It Home events are designed to be one-time-only events. Each event has a specific purpose to inspire, motivate and equip families to begin a specific faith skill in their home that they will continue doing forever. You don't stop doing family prayer when you learn how to do family service. The Take It Home events have a cumulative effect as each one adds to the others. Another reason why this Take It Home strategy is so effective is the fact that each individual faith skill has the ability to transform families. Just getting a family to pray together can transform that family for Christ.

I know from experience that not every family will latch on to every faith skill taught at the Take It Home events. In our church, we hold an event each year to teach parents of 2- to 3-year-olds how to bless their children each evening. I know that not every parent will do this, although some do. The next year, we teach parents how to do family devotions together. Again, I know that not every family will do this on a consistent basis, but some do. Therefore, we consistently give families the opportunity to bring Christ and Christlike living into their home. Even if you took a cynical view and claimed that over the course of 14 years and 14 Take It Home events a family only actively engages in 3 faith skills, I would point out that at least they are doing 3 more than they were before!

Pick whatever 3 skills you want from the list on page 84 and tell me that a family doing these skills regularly at home won't be changed for Christ. You can't! A family managing its money in a godly way will be changed. A family serving others together for Christ will be changed. A family that finds a Christian mentor to interact in the life of the family will be changed.

If a Take It Home event becomes just another activity at church, it won't have the type of impact needed to change families. But if you invest in Take It Home events so that they become experiences that inspire, motivate and equip parents to do these faith skills in the home, you'll see transformed families in the long run.

Ponder, Pray and Discuss

1. Are you a church "with" family ministry or are you a Faith@Home-focused church?

2. What do you like or dislike about the Faith@Home approach vs. the family ministry program approach?

3. Do you think your church members would be interested in learning more about practicing and nurturing faith at home?

4. In what ways could your church become more Faith@Home focused?

5. What are some of the challenges you face?

CHAPTER SUMMARY

- Reviewing where we've been.

- Why Faith@Home is a great opportunity and a great responsibility.

- Key #1: The senior pastor has to embrace the Faith@Home movement.

- Key #2: Be careful when you choose a name for the church initiative.

- Key #3: The church needs a Faith@Home-focused mission or vision—and a Faith@Home strategy to accomplish it.

- Key #4: A change in the way church is done requires confident humility.

- Key #5: Your church budget reflects whether your church treasures faith at home.

- Key #6: All church ministries should, naturally, be involved in carrying out your church's vision or strategy.

- Key #7: A Faith@Home champion will provide praise, prompting and provision for each church ministry so that every ministry remains focused on faith at home.

- Key #8: Preaching messages about faith at home should come naturally and be ongoing.

- Key #9: A long-term commitment to adopting and adapting the Faith@Home movement is necessary because results take time.

What Are the Keys to Becoming a Faith@Home-focused Church?

Jesus . . . loved fruit. Not the kind you pick off trees or vines,
but the kind that's evident in the life of a person whom He has changed.
He made very clear that the proof of people's faith is not in the informa-
tion they know or the religious gathering they attend, but in the way they
integrate what they know and believe into their everyday practices. . . .
The Lord encountered numerous people during His earthly tenure who
could quote Scripture or pretend they knew and loved Him. But His
reaction to them was always the same: "Show me the fruit."[1]
GEORGE BARNA

ANOTHER VOICE SAYS...

Brian Haynes, Associate Pastor, Kingsland Baptist Church
Katy, Texas
Creator of Legacy Milestones and author of
Shift: What It Takes to Finally Reach Families Today

Faith@Home is bigger than any one book or resource. At the same time, as a champion for the Faith@Home movement, Mark Holmen captures the essence of how God is leading churches to push faith back home as the primary place of spiritual influence.

My favorite section of the book is "Long-Term Commitment." This is a critical issue for church leaders everywhere. How do we develop ministry strategies that value Deuteronomy 6:4-9 as foundational as Matthew 28:18-20 (the Great Commission)? Mark answers that question by suggesting that we the Church need to embrace a Legacy Mindset. For too long we have defined success as the numbers inside our buildings today. Instead we should think of the generations. Holmen says, "As pastors and church leaders, we need to ask ourselves if we are willing to look beyond the quick fix and near future to a long-term goal with long-term impact."

He is exactly right! What will your church do to develop a Faith@Home ministry strategy? I am intrigued by the words of Nehemiah when he faced a seemingly insurmountable task: "Don't be afraid of them. Remember the Lord, who is great and awesome, and fight for your brothers, your sons and your daughters, your wives and your homes" (Neh. 4:14).

The Faith@Home movement is about the fight. Won't you join us!

Let's review the journey we've taken to this point. We've taken a critical look at what we're accomplishing (or, more accurately, not accomplishing) through the program-driven approach to ministry that has prevailed in churches over the past three to four decades. We've concluded that despite the fact that the church today is offering some of the best programs ever offered in and through the church, godly living—personified by prayer, Bible reading, devotions and faith talk—isn't taking place in homes today. Further, the Church has unintentionally enabled this to happen. Worse, unless something changes, people will continue to be engaged in church programs yet disengaged in their faith walk at home. This eventually results in overall disengagement.

As pastors and church leaders, we must ask ourselves if we want to enable this same pattern to continue or if we're willing to make some changes that will help families bring Christ back into the center of their homes. Now is our time to lead the Church. The personal decisions we make today will influence generations to come. This is both a great opportunity as well as a great responsibility.

The opportunity that God has brought us face to face with is a Faith@Home movement that He is leading to bring Christ and Christlike living back into the center of every household. The Faith@Home movement is not a specific program or ministry we need to launch but a strategy or approach that needs to be integrated throughout all the ministries of the church. Every ministry of the church has a role to play in equipping the home to be the primary place where faith is lived and nurtured.

So with that as the backdrop, let's take a look at some keys to becoming a Faith@Home-focused church.

Key #1: Senior Pastor Buy In

If You're Not the Senior Pastor

Probably the comment I hear the most when I speak about the Faith@Home movement across the world is "How do I get my senior pastor on board with this?" Let me reiterate that I do not believe senior pastors are not on board with this. I have yet to run across a senior pastor who has said, "Mark, I do not want my people to be Faith@Home focused!" What I do consistently hear from senior pastors is gratitude, because the Faith@Home methodology provided a practical way for them to address a problem they had seen in their churches. Here are just a few examples of the type of comments I constantly receive from senior pastors who attend a Faith@Home church seminar.

- Thank you for the Faith@Home conference. The concept of weaving ministries together has always been a desire of our church, and the theme of Faith@Home being intertwined throughout all ministries makes total sense!

• The Faith@Home initiative came at just the right time for our church. We immediately took up its vision. As a senior pastor, I had realized long ago that spiritual investment in kids is not primarily a church responsibility but should be in the hands of the parents. Our role as a church is to equip parents for this task. Thanks to [Faith@Home] we now have ideas to fulfill better this role. Also, we as pastors changed our ideas regarding kids, parents and also ourselves. We know that this is a long-term process, but we are already seeing results. We are grateful and motivated to continue on this path.

• Truly impacting—directional training. Thanks for your time and efforts! Eye opening—life changing. Ministry molding.

• As a pastor, I am thrilled about investing in the spiritual growth of people of different ages. I am convinced that growth happens spontaneously once the conditions are right. The local church has been created by God as a fertile soil to nurture His people into healthy spiritual living. Faith@Home immediately caught my attention, because it smells of a healthy spiritual climate. It helps me to simultaneously support spiritual growth for two different generations: parents and children. It is my firm conviction that Faith@Home effectively creates conditions for spiritual growth. For me, this is an important approach to spiritual leadership.

• Faith@Home met a crucial point in our church life, as the tendency seems to be global to delegate responsibilities from family to institutions. The inspiration and very practical support for families through the Faith@Home materials was urgent. It challenges parents who really seek the best for their kids but can't even imagine how much God entrusts them. I am amazed how the idea fits in our ministry. It enriched not only our church but also my personal relationship to my grandchildren, for it helped me to see not only my social and relational responsibility but also my spiritual impact beyond my children.

• Wonderful. Faith@Home resonated with my soul like a spring of fresh water in a desert of doing.

As you can see, senior pastors didn't need to be convinced; they simply needed to see a practical strategy for how to address the hypocritical one-hour-only Christianity all pastors face. Therefore, as you consider discussing Faith@Home with your senior pastor, please, by all means, do not go to him or her and say, "Here's a book you need to read and program you need to implement!" As a former senior pastor, hearing that makes my skin crawl—I was continually inundated with books I needed to read and programs I needed to implement.

Instead, as you bring the Faith@Home movement to the attention of your senior pastor, I encourage you to do so by attending to your pastor's heart, which is to see people live in an authentic 24/7 relationship with Jesus Christ. Every pastor wants that, and every pastor has a language they use for that. Some call it discipleship, others call it a lifestyle, and still others refer to it as being a fully devoted follower of Christ. Whatever your senior pastor calls it, use his or her own language when you discuss this subject. For example, you could say, "Excuse me, Pastor, but I came across something that is talking your language when it comes to discipleship [lifestyle or authentic Christianity]. I think this is the exact thing you have been talking about when you have mentioned that you want us to live in a fully devoted relationship with Jesus Christ."

Because Faith@Home fits somewhere into every senior pastor's heartbeat and vision for the church, getting your senior pastor to buy into it should be as simple as finding where the Faith@Home message fits within your pastor's passion and then approaching him or her from that direction.

Why have I spent so much space on the senior pastor? Because I believe that if a church is truly going to become a Faith@ Home-focused church, the senior pastor needs to understand and embrace the concept and approach. Now let me be clear: The implementation of the Faith@Home model can take place in a variety of ways and may take time, so don't be discouraged if your senior pastor isn't doing Faith@Home handsprings down the hallway. Senior pastors have a lot on their plate. But once your senior pastor firmly supports the Faith@Home methodology, some two-degree Faith@Home changes can be made. A few years from now, as people's lives begin to be transformed, word will spread in the community, and your senior pastor will be able to credit God for His hand in all of it (and just maybe your pastor will accept a few kudos for him- or herself—there was nothing I loved better as a senior pastor than when my staff members made me look good).

If You Are the Senior Pastor

Let me speak to you former senior pastor to senior pastor. Dear senior pastor, I realize the pressure you are under. You have people who want you to grow the church, expand the vision, reach more people, engage in more mission work, contribute to more community efforts and make your prayer ministry and worship life stronger. You have budgets, staffing and facility issues to deal with as well as funerals, weddings, hospital visits and, oh, by the way, a sermon you have to prepare and deliver with excellence every Sunday! It's not easy being a senior pastor today, especially in our quick-fix world where everybody wants instantaneous results. I wish I could say to you that launching a Faith@Home movement in your church will bring significant church growth instantaneously; but if that were the case, you would have already heard about it and tried it.

The truth of the matter is that instilling faith at home is a painstakingly slow process through which you will gradually, over time, change lifestyle behaviors that will, even further down the road, keep many children in the faith rather than disengaging from it. At the end of the day, you have to decide, as the called leader of your church, if the Faith@Home movement is something of God and if God is calling you to champion it in your church. I can't answer that for you. That's between you and God. I don't know how this book ended up in your hands or how you came to know about the Faith@Home movement, but I also do not believe in coincidences. I believe in "Godincidences," times when God is working in ways we cannot know, see or understand to guide us into the direction He wants us to go. I simply want to say thank you for giving your most precious commodity—your time—to read this book and consider if the Faith@Home movement is something God is calling you to be a part of.

If you have questions that you would like to ask a former senior pastor who led this movement in a church, know that I am here for you. Please give me a call or send me an email, and I will do my best to answer any questions or concerns you have (see my contact information at the back of the book). God bless you, my friend; and thank you for your commitment to leading God's people and serving His Church faithfully in spite of the trials, tribulations and challenges.

Key #2: Language Matters

At some point you are going to want to give a name to this initiative in your church and please hear me when I say this: Do not under any circumstances use the word "family" in your naming of this initiative. Why? Because the second you use the word family, anyone who doesn't have kids will tune you out and not get on board. I know this to be true, because we struggled for four years trying to get every member of our congregation involved in what we called our new approach to family ministry; and even though we explained multiple times that everyone was a part of a family, no matter how hard we tried, we simply couldn't get traction. Then when we were redoing our website, we decided to call this our Faith@Home initiative; and I'll never forget what Jim Tremaine, my pastor to seniors, said: "Oh, I like Faith@Home! That's something we can get behind." I looked at him and said,

"Jim, it's the same thing!" Then Jim responded, "Maybe so, but language matters."

Friends, I'm not saying you need to call this Faith@Home, but whatever you do, don't call it family ministry. I do have some good news for you. If you want to call it Faith@Home, you can, because in spite of strong counsel to the contrary, I have refused to trademark or copyright the term "Faith@Home". It seems to me that whenever a pastor has a good idea today, the pastor instantly copyrights it, trademarks it and makes money selling it. For me, the Faith@Home movement was a gift that was given to me from God; and I believe that when God gives you a gift, you are called to be a steward of it, not an owner. Therefore, I continue to steward the term "Faith@Home" and offer its free use to you and other church leaders all over the world.

Key #3: A Part of the Strategy of the Church

In a compelling talk titled "Four Things You Must Do," Bill Hybels, founding and senior pastor of Willow Creek Community Church, shared that one of the things people need most today is a clear and compelling vision. Hybels illustrated this with a story of a man from another church:

> I'll never forget a conversation I had with a churchgoing business guy. He had a huge heart for God at one time, but his heart for God was shrinking. He was in total frustration, and his frustration was leaking out all over the place. He pulled me aside at a conference and said, "Bill, will you meet with my pastor?"
>
> I said, "What for?"
>
> And he said, "To tell him to put a target on the wall. Any target on any wall! People like me just need some direction, some reason, any reason for staying in this game. I'm dying here. I'm dying here."
>
> And he was. He was perishing for lack of a vision.[2]

Another key to being a Faith@Home-focused church is identifying it as one of the core elements of your church strategy. When a church decides to become a faith at home-driven church, a clear vision has the potential to unite and ignite your congregation. Remember, a faith at home focus affects and engages everyone. A lot of church visions perish because they don't ground the vision through a faith at home set of lenses. The vision might be good, but it can't flourish because it hasn't been driven *home*—literally!

On the other hand, when a church adds the faith at home component to its vision, it becomes a vision that people can see, understand and apply to their own lives. This engages each individual personally in the vision. As a senior pastor, I love it when God provides something that creates unity, engagement and positive momentum in my congregation!

Every church has a mission, vision and/or strategy. For some, it looks like a baseball diamond. For others, it might be five Gs, four Cs, or some other creative acronym. If your church wants to be a Faith@Home-focused church, while that goal doesn't necessarily have to appear in your mission statement, it should definitely appear in your vision and/or strategy.

At Ventura Missionary Church, our mission statement was "to introduce people to a growing relationship with Jesus Christ." Our Faith@Home focus did not appear in the mission statement but it came out in our strategy for how we fulfill this mission. Essentially, we asked ourselves, *How are we going to fulfill this mission of introducing people to a growing relationship with Jesus Christ?* For us, it came down to four goals for each church member:

1. *You and Jesus:* At the end of the day, Christianity comes down to a decision you are going to make regarding Jesus. To put it in "churchy" language, you are a sinner in need of a Savior, and Jesus has come as your Savior to give you life and life everlasting. Therefore, you need to make a decision regarding Jesus and as a church we are going to do everything we can to lead you to accept Him as your Lord and Savior.

2. *You and Faith@Home:* Now that you have accepted Jesus as your Lord and Savior, it is time for you to live in a 24/7 relationship with Him. We are not called to be one-hour-at-church-only hypocritical Christians. We are called to invite Him into our daily lives, which begins by opening the door of our homes and saying, "Come in, Jesus, and live with me." The Faith@Home movement is about helping you to live in a loving relationship with Jesus Christ 24 hours a day, 7 days a week.

3. *You and the Church:* Now that you have welcomed Jesus into your home, you need to recognize that Jesus also has a Bride that you are called to know, love and serve. We as Christians are not called to simply do church: We are called to live in a loving relationship with the church, joyfully and obediently loving and serving her.

4. *You and the World:* Finally, God has created you with unique gifts for a purpose that God has to use you to make a difference in the world. As fully devoted followers of Christ, we are called to go and be "little Christs" in our homes, neighborhoods, community and world.

I share this with you so that you can see that Faith@Home is not the only thing VMC emphasizes as a church. Yes, it is a Faith@Home-focused church ("You and Faith@Home"), but it is also an evangelical/lost-people-matter church ("You and Jesus") and a church where being connected into community through small groups is important ("You and the Church"); and it is a missional church ("You and the World").

VMC's strategy for doing church in the manner to which God has called it is to emphasize those four things across every ministry of the church. *Every* ministry is expected to introduce people to Christ, to instill Faith@Home, to get people connected into the church and to empower people to go out and make a difference in the world. Pastors and church leaders are hired and fired based on

NURSERY	CHILDREN	YOUTH	ADULT	SENIORS
You & Jesus (Evangelism)				
You & Fatih@Home (Discipleship)				
You & the World (Missionality)				
You & the Church (Small Groups)				

their ability to do these four things in their ministry area. When I was senior pastor, I evaluated my ministry leaders at the end of each year by asking the following series of questions:

1. How many people did your ministry introduce to Christ this year? How do you plan to continue to accomplish this next year?
2. How did your ministry help people live out their faith at home? How do you plan to continue to accomplish this next year?
3. How did your ministry get people connected into the church, loving and serving her? How do you plan to continue to accomplish this next year?
4. How did your ministry get people out making a difference in the community or world? How do you plan to continue to accomplish this next year?

As you can see, Faith@Home was not the only thing we did as a church, but it was one of our core strategy components. Now, I'm not saying that your church has to copy VMC's way of doing things. This is just one way to work out your strategy so that you accomplish your mission or vision. The basic point is that the people of your church, especially the staff, need to know where and how the Faith@Home focus fits into your overall mission or vision as a church.

Key #4: Confident Humility

In his research for *Breakout Churches,* Thom Rainer discovered that pastors who were able to successfully lead a breakout movement in their previously plateaued churches shared one key quality and character trait. He summed it up in two words: "confident humility."[3]

It took me awhile to sink my teeth into that one, because you don't usually see those two words together. For me, "confident humility" means that senior pastors leading a Faith@Home movement in our churches must lead this movement in the full confidence that it is of God and exactly what God desires of us. I have complete confidence that Christ wants to reside in the center of every home, and I believe His heart breaks over the fact that most Christians who attend our churches aren't engaged in Christlike living at home.

Knowing that the present state of faith at home is not how God intended it to be makes me *confident* that I can and should boldly lead a Faith@Home movement in my ministry or church. At the same time, I stand in complete *humility,* humbled by the daunting task of trying to reestablish Christ and Christlike living in the center of every home.

Leading a Faith@Home movement definitely is daunting. It isn't and won't be easy. To be honest, it's somewhat overwhelming. Getting faith back to being practiced and nurtured in every home isn't something we can fix quickly or measure easily. Yet that itself is even more motivation to come humbly before the Lord to seek His face, strength and ability to do something we can't do ourselves.

Key #5: Financial Commitment

Jesus said, "For where your treasure is, there your heart will be also" (Matt. 6:21). We can easily adapt this verse to apply to the church as well: "Where your budget is, there your commitment as a church will be also." If the church is going to make a significant impact on what's happening in the home, we must commit equally significant resources from our church budgets to staffing and resourcing Faith@Home.

Unfortunately, in most churches we spend a large percentage of our budget on programs and resources that primarily get used at church but hardly any funds on resources that the family can use in the home. I challenge you to look at your current church budget and ask yourself, *How much money are we spending as a church to equip the home to be the primary place where faith is nurtured?* If the home is more influential than the church, shouldn't we be devoting more resources to what is more effective and God-ordained?

When I served as the youth and family ministry pastor at Calvary Lutheran Church, we spent as much money on resources that we gave away at Take It Home events for families to use in the home as we did on Sunday School curriculum. Let me state that again! *We spent as much money on resources that we gave away at Take It Home events for families to use in the home as we did on Sunday School curriculum.* Obviously, this constituted a major commitment that took many years to build up to.

When I came to serve as senior pastor of Ventura Missionary Church, I knew that we would have to increase our financial commitment to family ministry. On the Sunday that I preached the "Home as Church, Too" message, I painted a picture of some of the steps we would take to equip parents to pass on the faith to their children. I also told the congregation that these ideas needed financial support that wasn't in our budget. I concluded the message by giving the congregation a chance to make an above-and-beyond financial gift to our new faith at home effort. The congregation responded by giving more than $30,000. This became the seed money we used to fund our new family ministry efforts until we could build it into our annual budgets.

I know that church budgets are tight. But I also know that people will give to a ministry that they sense will make a difference. If you cast a faith at home vision and attach to it the practical resources you need to help families reestablish the home as the primary place where faith is nurtured, the resources will come. In fact, I've discovered that it's easier to get funding for your faith at home movement than just about any other item in your church budget!

Key #6: Get All Ministries Involved

One common mistake that inhibits the Faith@Home movement from getting the traction it needs to fully flourish in a church is pigeonholing the movement under the umbrella of children's ministry. As previously stated, the Faith@Home effort is something every ministry should be participating in:

- Women's ministry should be equipping women to be godly women at home.

- Men's ministry should be equipping men to be godly men at home.

- Seniors' ministry should be encouraging and engaging seniors to be meddling parents and grandparents in the spiritual lives of their children and grandchildren.

- Small-group ministry should be used as a perfect outlet for Faith@Home training by using small-group studies focused on practicing faith at home. This applies to whichever types of small groups your church hosts (for men, women, parents, singles, etc.).

- Outreach ministry should help individuals get engaged in serving others in your community. The VMC outreach pastor came up with an at-home-focused approach called "Trash Can Make a Difference." Essentially, each household takes a trash can and places it in a prominent place in their home. Then each month a different community cause is identified, and each family is responsible for filling the trash can with the items needed for that community cause.

At the end of the month, the items from all the trash cans are taken to the local agency whose cause is being supported that month. For example, one month canned goods for a local food pantry are collected and the next month baby items for the local pregnancy shelter are collected.

Limiting Faith@Home activities to children's ministry is a disservice to the other ministries of your church. One of the best ways I've discovered to foster broader church support for the movement is to hold a one-day Faith@Home summit meeting (see the Faith@Home summit meeting outline found in appendix 3). The purpose of such a meeting is to remind your ministry leaders of the biblical mandate for the practice of faith at home, as well as to create a sense of urgency and ownership for all the ministries of your church. The Faith@Home summit meeting can serve as a catalyst for your church's journey toward becoming a Faith@Home-focused church, as each ministry assumes a part to play in making your church's mission or vision happen.

Key #7: Identify and Empower a Faith@Home Champion

Another key to being a Faith@Home-focused church is having a Faith@Home champion (or team of champions) who you empower to go into every ministry to praise, prompt and provide ideas and resources so that each of your ministries will maintain a Faith@Home focus. In some churches the Faith@Home champion is a lay leader, while in others the duties of the Faith@Home champion become part of a staff person's job description (to see how Faith@Home can be woven into a job description, see appendix 1). The key in all scenarios is empowering the Faith@Home champion to facilitate the Faith@Home discussion in every ministry area. Let me give you an example of how such a champion (or team) functions.

Margaret and Kris are two precious women who are prayer champions at Ventura Missionary Church. They were prayer champions before I arrived as the senior pastor, and they will continue to be prayer champions at VMC until the day Jesus either calls them home or He returns. One of the things that I knew would happen every year is that Margaret and Kris would set up a time to meet with me; and every time at this annual meeting, they would do the following three things:

1. *Praise*: The first thing they would do is praise me for all the ways I had championed prayer over the past year. They would literally pull out a notepad of paper and methodically take me through a list of things I had done. At first, I thought they were keeping track of me, as if to see whether I did enough or the right number of things; but their spirit was one of genuine support. They simply wanted to praise and thank me for all the things I had done. By the time they were done, I felt as if I had done a good job championing prayer as a senior pastor.

2. *Prompt:* Following the time of praise, Margaret and Kris would ask me, "So, Pastor, what are you planning to do to champion prayer this year?" I loved this question, because it always prompted me to think about how I was going to continue to keep prayer on the radar of our church in the year ahead.

3. *Provide*: Margaret and Kris would ask me one final thing: "Is there anything we can do to help you champion prayer, Pastor?" Some years I didn't need help, but there were also years where I needed a new book on prayer or a sermon series on prayer. All I had to do was mention my need; and within days, I would be provided with new books on prayer or a new sermon series on prayer!

Key #8: Preach Faith@Home

Another key for Faith@Home-focused churches comes down to how they approach preaching Faith@Home messages. Unfortunately, many pastors simply set aside one Sunday a year for a family-focused service or sermon. Some might even go as far as having a family-focused sermon *series* each year, thinking this will challenge families to bring Christ into their home.

I'm sorry to be the one to have to point this out, but one sermon or sermon series a year will not get the faith at home job done any more than telling your new puppy one time to quit tinkling on the carpet! (My mother-in-law uses the term "tinkling" because it's less offensive than the other word.) Just as training a puppy takes a lot of repetition, so too does the consistent reinforcement of faith at home through your preaching and teaching.

Instilling Faith@Home requires repetition, which we see in Deuteronomy (which, by the way, means "repetition of the law"). The Israelites needed constant repetition of the Law, and so do we. Therefore, each sermon you give should have an eye toward how the godly truth, attribute or insight you're preaching about can be transferred into the way people live at home. This really shouldn't be difficult; in fact, it should be natural. I didn't need to try to find ways to fit Faith@Home into my messages because Faith@Home is an overarching theme throughout Scripture. I even used Faith@Home language at weddings and funerals!

How does Faith@Home fit at a funeral? Think about it for a minute, and then I'll tell you how I did it. When I led the funeral service of a lifelong follower of Christ who had impacted the lives of the people in attendance through his or her faithfulness, I would say, "Now do you see why we emphasize Faith@Home? How many of you here were impacted or influenced by this person's faith? How many of you would like to have a funeral filled with people bearing testimony to the impact your faith made on their life? Then go and live out your faith at home like this person did."

Does this mean I should never do a sermon series on the family or Faith@Home? No, that's not what I'm saying, because sermon series are great catalysts for a Faith@Home initiative.

Steve Stroope, senior pastor of Lakepointe Church in Dallas, Texas, has done a great job doing this:

> At Lake Pointe Church, one of the ways we have decided to keep the Faith@Home movement before our people is to have fall and spring campaigns. A campaign consists of drilling down on one aspect of Faith@Home that provides more of a major focus rather than a shotgun approach. Our intention is to encourage and reinforce a habit each time we have a campaign. For example, our first campaign was Praying@Home, in which we encouraged each home to be a 7-5-2 family where everyone in the home committed to pray for their family members 7 times a week, pray with their family members 5 times a week, and for spouses to pray with each other twice a week after sharing intimate and detailed prayer requests.
>
> We had close to 9,000 people make commitments to be a 7-5-2 family for the following 120 days. We provided prayer calendars for all of our grade-school kids in which they could mark each time they prayed for their family, each time they prayed together as a family, and when Mom and Dad prayed together. Another campaign was our Serving Together campaign where once again we asked everyone to commit to be involved in at least one serving project a month for the following 120 days. We then provided a list of serving opportunities in which family members of all ages could minister together.
>
> A third campaign was Blessing Your Family, in which we encouraged family members to affirm one another. During each campaign, we provided printed materials with specific information, such as recommended books and CDs. In addition, at least one message on the topic was preached in each campaign, and commitment cards were distributed that called for the specific commitment in writing.

Obviously, sermon series like this will propel your Faith@ Home initiative forward, but when your preaching and teaching has ongoing Faith@Home references throughout the year, you'll continue to fan the flame week after week. This greatly increases your chances of igniting the type of fire for Christ that you want to see in every individual you serve.

Key #9: Long-Term Commitment

One thing that continually amazes me about our culture is how quick-fix-oriented we've become. We want instant gratification. If a professional sports coach doesn't lead his team to a championship within a few years, he gets fired. A recent commercial I saw boldly proclaimed through a very annoying hard-rock jingle, "I want it all! I want it all! I want it now!" We eat fast food, drive fast cars, have the fastest computers with the fastest Internet connection, and we attempt to lose weight as fast as we can by drinking Slim Fast! Often, our culture determines the success of a program or product solely by the amount of time it takes to produce results.

Remember the TV show *Seinfeld* from a few years back? In one of my favorite episodes, Kramer walks into Jerry's apartment with his latest million-dollar idea and says, "Jerry, you've heard of the 10-minute abs video that promises you great abs in 10 minutes, haven't you?"

"Yes, I have," Jerry replies.

Kramer then excitedly announces, "I'm coming out with a new video that's going to make me rich. It's called 9-minute abs. You can't tell me that if my 9-minute abs video is sitting on the shelf next to their 10-minute abs video that everyone won't buy mine."

Jerry then responds, "That makes sense, Kramer. But I have one question for you. What if someone comes out with an 8-minute abs video?"

Kramer, stunned and totally taken aback by the thought, simply responds, "No one would do that. Everyone knows you can't get great abs in 8 minutes!"

As funny and ridiculous as that episode was, it illustrates what our culture has become. If we can achieve results faster, we'll go for it.

Major Results Take Time

In many ways, as pastors we get caught up in this same reality and feel the same pressure. If we don't produce instantaneous results—measured typically by increased attendance, new programs, better giving and building programs—then we feel that we might need to consider a new calling. There's always another church that is growing faster, preaching better and being more creative and innovative than we are. If our church isn't bursting at the seams and hitting record numbers every year, we can easily feel that we're failing.

Instead of focusing on where the Lord uniquely calls us to go as a church, we look across the street or halfway around the world at another church and say, "That's what we need to do here!" The chase continues to find the next innovative program or dynamic staff person who can provide that quick fix and instantaneous result we feel pressured to accomplish. As church consultant Thom Rainer writes, "Churches and their lay leaders can be incredibly demanding of, if not vicious to, pastors. In my consulting ministry with the Rainer Group, I often deal with lay leaders who treat pastors like CEOs and expect immediate results of them."[4]

Change Takes Time

About four years into my ministry as senior pastor of Ventura Missionary Church, I had to face this reality at a board and staff retreat. Let me provide a little background information so that you can better understand what was taking place.

VMC experienced exponential growth in the 1980s and early 1990s as the church grew from 80 people to more than 1,500. At the same time, the city of Ventura grew from roughly 40,000 people to more than 100,000. When I arrived, the church had been on a 3-year decline, with some 850 people attending worship services. Due to some strong anti-growth campaigns that undermined new housing development plans, the city of Ventura had also stopped growing. In spite of this, the church had a strong desire to grow and reach the lost for Christ.

As a young and naïve pastor, I was excited to be a part of a church that wanted to grow. I believed we could easily turn the ship around and become a growing congregation again. However, this turned out to be a much more difficult task than I had realized.

During the first two years, we were able to stop the downward spiral and grow to more than 1,000. But then we plateaued for the next two years. During this plateau time, we became more committed to our faith at home focus and initiated many of our Take It Home events. In the first years of this new vision, as is often the case, the Take It Home events were works in progress. Still, families began to experience for the first time the opportunity to pray, read the Bible, lead devotions, bless their children and do family service projects together. We started to hear stories of how moms and dads were doing these ideas at home.

As the climate at VMC began to change, each ministry took more ownership in the Faith@Home-focused vision we had established. Then we were asked to be one of the first 200 churches to participate in the Reveal survey through the Willow Creek Association. In this survey, four "Personal Spiritual Practice" questions were asked that dialed in to Faith@Home behavior. When we received the results, we discovered that we were twice the national average in those four categories! The next Sunday, I stood before the church and said, "I have some good news and some bad news. The good news is that when it comes to personal spiritual practices at home, as a church we are ahead of the curve as we are twice the national average." Everyone cheered. "But now the bad news. The national average was 21 percent and our average is 47 percent, which means that in spite of our efforts, we still have less than half of our people engaged in Faith@Home living, so if you think this emphasis on Faith@Home is going away, it's not going to happen until we get to 100 percent!" To my amazement everyone stood and applauded. We were in this for the long haul!

As pastors and church leaders, we need to ask ourselves if we are willing to look beyond the quick fix and near future to a long-term goal with long-term impact.

Ponder, Pray and Discuss

1. Is your senior pastor committed to making Faith@Home one of the top priorities in your church?

2. Is Faith@Home integrated into your church's mission or vision and in the strategy your church uses to accomplish the church's goal?

3. What percentage of your budget is committed to providing resources families can use in the home? Is that enough to get the job done?

4. Are all the ministries of the church incorporated and committed to your Faith@Home efforts?

5. Is Faith@Home a consistent emphasis in your preaching and teaching?

6. Is your church ready to make a long-term commitment to advocating Faith@Home, recognizing that there's no quick fix for the transformation that needs to occur within households?

CHAPTER SUMMARY

- Trap #1: The Faith@Home movement is a revolution (actually, it's an evolution).

- Trap #2: The Faith@Home movement is an all or nothing proposition (actually, it should start small).

- Trap #3: What we are currently doing is ineffective (actually, it's been incredibly effective).

- Trap #4: Only excellence is good enough (actually, good enough is good enough).

- Trap #5: Only a large church can pull this off (actually, church size doesn't matter).

- Trap #6: One Take It Home event a year isn't enough (actually, one event can be very effective).

- Trap #7: The Faith@Home movement guarantees success (actually, odds only greatly improve, although that's an important "only"!).

- Trap #8: Support of the senior pastor is a necessity (actually, it's not).

- Trap #9: Practicing Faith@Home isn't for singles (actually, a person's marital status doesn't matter).

- Trap #10: It's too late for seniors to practice faith at home (actually, age doesn't matter).

- Trap #11: After several years, you'll need something new (actually, believers need to remain in the movement).

- Future wins: Faith@Home brings unity; stronger mission, vision and strategy; short-term results; and long-term, multigenerational impact.

5

What Are the Traps to Avoid, and What Would We Win?

A mark of leaders, an attribute that puts them in a position to show the way for others, is that they are better than most at pointing the direction. As long as one is leading, one always has a goal. It may be a goal arrived at by group consensus, or the leader, acting on inspiration, may simply have said, "Let's go this way." But the leader always knows what it is and can articulate it for any who are unsure. By clearly stating and restating the goal the leader gives certainty to others who may have difficulty in achieving it for themselves.[1]
ROBERT GREENLEAF

ANOTHER VOICE SAYS...
Arthur Jenkins, Senior Pastor, Saint James Church
James Island, South Carolina

When I first heard the teaching of family-based Christian discipleship and the Faith@Home movement, it didn't strike me as a senior pastor; it struck my heart as a father. The senior pastor in me could maybe have convinced myself that we had *not* been doing discipleship incorrectly for the last 50 years, but my father's heart told me otherwise. As I faced the conviction of the words of Deuteronomy 6 and Psalm 78, words I had read many times, I wanted to run from the conviction in any way possible—blame, rationalization, anything but facing it. By God's grace I responded the only way I could as a disciple of Jesus. I repented. First I went to my family. I have two adult daughters, both of whom I can say are fine Christian young ladies. They listened to my repentance, my sorrow, with love and interest. The most powerful Christian witness a parent can offer a child is confession and repentance. The most powerful way I could tell my family that this is important was to repent.

After starting with my own family, I turned to my church family and again did the only thing I could do. I repented. I told the church that I had been wrong for 20 years. I had assumed that our church-based discipleship programs were working. I told them I was sorry and asked for their forgiveness. I explained that I was tired of hearing parents with adult children say, "But I did everything right. My child was in Sunday School. They served in worship and went to youth group and yet now, they don't darken the church door." The transparency and humility necessary for public repentance are hard, but it is not as hard as hearing that.

Obviously, not everyone signed on to their new role with their family, but they did understand this is important.

I've been privileged to work with pastors who've led the Faith@ Home movement in churches of every different size and affiliation as well as from different countries from across the world. As a result, I've had the opportunity to experience and see things that can hinder as well as encourage church leaders as they direct their church to achieve the goal of becoming more Faith@Home focused.

In the following sections, I am going to share 11 of the traps that I have discovered through personal experience over the years that I hope will help prevent you from making the same mistakes. Please note that because the Faith@Home movement is a work in progress, this certainly isn't an exhaustive list. However, I also urge you not to minimize the importance of these traps—understanding these will be critically important to the success of the Faith@ Home movement in your congregation.

Trap #1: The Faith@Home Movement Is a Revolution

Many people today like to use the term "revolution" to describe their latest idea or ministry paradigm shift. For some reason, I have never found the term "revolution" to be helpful. "Pastor, it's time to lead a revolution in our church! It's time for the Faith@Home revolution!" To me, this sounds like we are going to war, which implies casualties, but who cares? God will prevail! I don't know about you, but this warlike approach doesn't appeal to me, and it instantly puts some people on the defensive, making them feel as if the things they love about the Church are being attacked. Why do we need to make instant enemies of some people or put people on the defensive by using a warlike term? Instead, I describe the Faith@Home movement as an evolution. It's the next thing that God is calling us to as a Church that continues to evolve as we faithfully follow Him. Now that we have some great programs in our churches, it's time to leverage those programs to bring Christ and Christlike living back into the home. That's evolutionary not revolutionary.

Trap #2: Do It All or Do Nothing

We live in a day where we want it all right away. We have no patience, and unless we can offer our people the full smorgasbord of opportunities, we feel as if we are failing. We also love to compare ourselves to others: "If only we were like them, had what they had, did what they did, offered what they offer . . ." And when it comes to Faith@Home, we think that the senior pastor and every ministry, along with the rest of the staff, have to immediately jump on board, doing Faith@Home handstands while we instantly provide everything, including an over-the-top budget, in order to produce all 13 Take It Home events during the year. Oh, and lest I forget, we also need a new Faith@Home pastor and Take It Home room with large-screen TVs, and we need this all in 30 days or less!

Friends, even though I served in a church that offered more than 13 Take It Home events in a designated Take It Home room that had a large-screen TV, you need to know that we didn't start this way. During our first year, we hosted three Take It Home events in the worst rooms in the church. We started doing what we could with what we had, and we continued to grow our Faith@Home emphasis slowly. It didn't happen overnight. It took awhile to get all the staff on board; and we had to slowly build the shift changes into our budget, so we could provide the Faith@Home resources we wanted to provide.

You need to avoid the trap of thinking you can do it all right away. Take your time and do what you can initially; then build out from there.

Trap #3: Current Efforts Are Ineffective

I think we need to be careful as we champion Faith@Home to make sure that we don't give the impression that what we are doing in children's, youth or family ministry or in any other of our programs is ineffective. Many people have given their blood, sweat and tears to make the current ministries the very best they can be. Friends, I don't believe that our current efforts are ineffective. I praise God for the ministries and programs, the Bible camps and the retreats—everything local churches have done has been incredibly effective at helping all ages and types of people know the love of Jesus Christ. I know, however, that everything we do could be even more effective if a Faith@Home focus were included.

Trap #4: Only Excellence Is Good Enough

If you came to Ventura Missionary Church during any given week, you wouldn't see some incredible program with dancing elephants or a building that absolutely wows you. In fact, there is nothing fancy or jaw dropping about any of the Faith@Home things that are done there. Yet the Faith@Home emphasis is something you would run into throughout every ministry of the church—from the Take It Homework in the bulletins to the Take It Home events being led in the upper room behind the sanctuary to the men's dinner speaker who is focusing on some faith skill. The movement is simply woven into everything that happens at VMC.

Recently, a group of pastors from different churches in Canada came to VMC to meet with us and witness a Take It Home event. At the end of the weekend, I'll never forget their comment: "What we love about what you're doing is the fact that there really isn't anything fancy about it. It's not like you need a fancy facility or charismatic leader to make it happen. Please don't take this wrong; but there is nothing spectacular about your church facility, yet the way you have woven the Faith@Home vision into how you do church is truly spectacular. This is something any church can do and every church needs to do."

In the 1990s, there was a big emphasis on making sure that everything done in church was done with excellence. While I believe in striving for excellence in all we do, I have also discovered that there is a "good enough" bar that allows us to realize that we can offer something very effective, without waiting for excellence, as long as we can do it good enough. Let me give you an example.

When we launched our first Take It Home event, we decided to go with an event that focused on family blessing for parents of three-year-olds. To be honest, this was a no-brainer for us, because I had a powerful, tear-jerking, motivational testimony about the impact the ritual of blessing had made in our life, plus we had a great resource to provide on blessings. Dave set up the event to begin in the morning with a puppet show to be watched by both parents and their children. After the show, the children were to be escorted to another room for a snack, which would allow me time to tell the powerful blessing story that would motivate the parents to want to start blessing their children as soon as they were brought back into the room.

The event began as we had expected, and the puppet show was going very well with the children watching with glee as the parents sat behind them. Unfortunately, the unforeseen then happened. The puppet show ended innocently enough with some confetti being thrown over the curtain to fall down on top of the children's heads. While almost all the children thought this was great fun, one three-year-old thought this meant the sky was falling and the world, as he knew it, was coming to an end! He instantly started to scream and cry. All of the other children who had been okay up until this time now realized the error of their ways, and they too began to join in the chorus of terror and tears. There was absolutely no chance of the children being escorted to another room for a snack because all of them were now being consoled by their parents.

Dave looked at me, not knowing what to do, and said, "Just go ahead and tell your story." I remembered thinking to myself, *Are you kidding me? This has no chance of success. No parent is going to listen as they are trying to keep their children in the room!* But seeing that there was no other choice, I simply stepped up and attempted to tell the story. Let's just say it went as well as I thought it would; in other words, it bombed. No one was paying attention, and the event never got any better. Dave and I later laughed as we went to my office, agreeing that this had to be easily the worst Take It Home event of all time; and if there is a good enough bar, we didn't come close to hitting it!

About six months later, Dave came into my office and excitedly said, "Mark, you'll never guess what happened last night. Do you remember that really bad Take It Home event we did on blessings?"

"How could I forget!" I replied.

Dave continued, "Last night I was asked to attend a small group, and all they did was compliment me for that Take It Home event. They said that they have been blessing their kids ever since, and each of the dads said it had become their favorite part of the day!" Dave and I had been taught a lesson. Sometimes, even not good enough in our eyes is good enough in God's!

That being said, please accept the fact that your first several Take It Home events will probably be average at best. Don't be surprised if they don't go well, but don't get discouraged either. We have an enemy who is not going to give up his turf easily. Keep pressing on, and your second year will be better, and by year three, you will really have something good going. Beginning with your third year, you'll have the ability to use some of your own people, from previous years, to share their testimonies—and that is really fun! So hang in there, and remember that sometimes good enough is all you need!

Trap #5: Only a Large Church Can Pull This Off

Many times we run into programs or movements that are clearly large-church oriented, but I am proud to say that this is not the case for the Faith@Home movement. As someone who has led this in small, medium and large churches, I can say without hesitation that it is easier to launch a Faith@Home movement in a small- or medium-sized church than it is in a large church. Why? Because in a large church you have more ministry areas and staff to get on board before you can make major moves forward. I have worked on-again, off-again with one very large church that has been laboring to become Faith@Home focused for over seven years! Now, this doesn't mean that a large church can't pull this off—Lakepoint Church in Dallas, Texas, and Beaverton Foursquare Church in Portland, Oregon, have clearly shown that this is not the case—but I wanted to make sure that everyone understands that the Faith@Home movement can work in any sized church.

Trap #6: One Take It Home Event a Year Isn't Enough

"Are you telling me that it can be as simple as one event a year? Can one event a year really make a difference?" Those are two of the most commonly asked questions I receive, and the answer to both, to put it quite simply, is yes. George Barna has described the Faith@Home movement as revolutionarily simple. It's revolutionary in its impact, yet it is simple in its application. So can one event a year really make a difference? You tell me.

I remember attending our first Take It Home event when my daughter was three. The event focused on blessing and I was brought face to face with the story and testimony of Rolf Garborg, author of *The Family Blessing*.[2] Rolf told us that he had started a ritual of saying a blessing over his daughter every evening. When she was an infant, he would go into her room as she was sleeping and say, "May the Lord continue to bless you and keep you. May the Lord continue to make His face shine on you and be gracious to you. May the Lord continue to look upon you with favor and give you peace. In the name of the Father, and the Son and the Holy Spirit. I love you. Amen."

As Rolf's daughter grew older, he continued the blessing ritual, even through her teenage years. He admits that during one period of time when she was a teenager, he would again wait until she was asleep to give her the blessing. But he kept up the ritual.

Rolf and his wife dreaded the day when they would have to leave their daughter at college. To make it through that day, they came up with a plan to unload her stuff, quickly say their goodbyes in the dorm room, grab each other's hand and head for the car with no looking back. The plan worked to perfection—until they were almost to their car. In the distance behind them, they heard their daughter cry, "Mom! Dad! Wait!"

Rolf and his wife stopped in their tracks and turned around to see their daughter come running up after them. With tears in her eyes, she said, "You forgot to bless me." Right there in the parking lot, they huddled together and said, "May the Lord continue to bless you and keep you. May the Lord continue to make His face shine on you and be gracious to you. May the Lord continue to look upon you with favor and give you peace. In the name of the Father, and the Son and the Holy Spirit. I love you. Amen."

Guess what Maria and I started doing immediately after we heard this story? Every evening before Malyn went to bed, Maria would repeat this same blessing to her. Even if we were separated for an evening, Maria would share the blessing over the phone. There were even occasions when Malyn said, "Don't forget to bless me!"

My daughter is now a teenager, and before she goes to bed she comes to me for prayer and to her mom for her blessing. And whenever I travel, which is fairly frequently, my daughter will send me a text message (that's how teenaged girls communicate with their dads nowadays) that reads, "Daddy, as u travel may the Lord bless u and keep u. May He make His face shine on you and b gracious 2 u. May He look upon u with favor and give u peace. In the name of the Father and the Son and the Holy Spirit. Amen." What makes things even better for me is knowing that she is growing up with this as normal. Tell me she won't be blessing our grandchildren, even though I may not let her date until she's 30!

Now, you just try to tell me that one event can't make a difference!

Trap #7: The Faith@Home Movement Guarantees Success

One of the traps we need to avoid is giving the impression that if parents do these faith skills in the home it will guarantee that their children will never stray. I wish we could say that, but we can't. However, we can tell parents that the odds increase greatly that their kids will not stray, although this isn't a guarantee.

I think every parent wants the best for their children. We all want our children to avoid drugs, alcohol, violence, gangs and promiscuous sexual activity. We want them to get good grades and maintain a healthy lifestyle. We want everything good for our children, but every parent wonders how to accomplish this. A person who had a great impact on my life as a youth and family pastor and as a parent was a man by the name of Merton Strommen. Mert was a research scientist who cared deeply about children. One day he asked himself a simple question: *Why do some children turn out good while others do not?* Obviously there was no simple answer to this question, so Mert, founder of Search Institute, put his research team to work. After years of research was collected and evaluated, Search Institute identified 30 developmental assets (this list has since grown to 40) that a child needs to succeed.[3]

What made the research so eye opening was the fact that when the assets are nurtured in children, many of the problems that we worry about among youth are reduced. The research revealed that the more assets a child has in his or her life, the less likely that child is to become involved in at-risk behaviors like illicit drugs, alcohol use, early sexual activity, violence, and so forth (see the charts on pages 133-134).

The results also showed that the more assets a child had in his or her life the more likely they will do well in school and be involved in other positive activities (see the charts below).

Assets in Relation to At-Risk Behaviors

Problem Alcohol Use		Illicit Drug Use		Sexual Activity		Violence	
(Three or more uses in the last month or got drunk one or more times in past two weeks.)		(Three or more uses in the past year.)		(Sexual intercourse, three or more times, lifetime.)		(Three or more acts of fighting, hitting, injuring a person, or using a weapon in the past year.)	
If 0-10 Assets	49%	If 0-10 Assets	39%	If 0-10 Assets	32%	If 0-10 Assets	61%
If 11-20 Assets	27%	If 11-20 Assets	18%	If 11-20 Assets	21%	If 11-20 Assets	38%
If 21-25 Assets	11%	If 21-25 Assets	6%	If 21-25 Assets	11%	If 21-25 Assets	19%
If 26-30 Assets	3%	If 26-30 Assets	<1%	If 26-30 Assets	3%	If 26-30 Assets	7%

Note: Finding based on surveys of over 217,000 sixth- to twelfth-grade youth in 318 communities and 33 states during the 1999-2000 school year. The same kind of impact is evident with many other problem behaviors, including tobacco use, depression and attempted suicide, antisocial behavior, school problems, driving and alcohol, and gambling.[4]

Succeeds in School		Exhibits Leadership		Maintains Good Health		Volunteer Service (Volunteers one or more hours per week)	
If 0-10 Assets	3%	If 0-10 Assets	50%	If 0-10 Assets	26%	If 0-10 Assets	15%
If 11-20 Assets	13%	If 11-20 Assets	65%	If 11-20 Assets	47%	If 11-20 Assets	34%
If 21-25 Assets	28%	If 21-25 Assets	77%	If 21-25 Assets	69%	If 21-25 Assets	57%
If 26-30 Assets	51%	If 26-30 Assets	85%	If 26-30 Assets	89%	If 26-30 Assets	75%

Note: Findings based on surveys of over 217,000 sixth- to twelfth-grade youth in 318 communities and 33 states during the 1999-2000 school year.[5]

The first time I looked over these results and saw the impact these assets had, I instantly remember saying to myself, *I want to make sure my daughter has 26 to 30 of these assets in her life.* I think every parent would feel the same way.

Forty Developmental Assets

Search Institute has identified the following building blocks of healthy development that help young people grow up healthy, caring and responsible.

EXTERNAL ASSETS

Category	Asset Name and Definition
Support	1. **Family Support**—Family life provides high levels of love and support.
	2. **Positive family communication**—Young person and her or his parent(s) communicate positively, and young person is willing to seek advice and counsel from parent(s).
	3. **Other adult relationships**—Young person receives support from three or more nonparent adults.
	4. **Caring neighborhood**—Young person experiences caring neighbors.
	5. **Caring school climate**—School provides a caring, encouraging environment.
	6. **Parent involvement in schooling**—Parent(s) is actively involved in helping young person succeed in school.
Empowerment	7. **Community values youth**—Young person perceives that adults in the community value youth.
	8. **Youth as resources**—Young people are given useful roles in the community.
	9. **Service to others**—Young person serves in the community one hour or more per week.
	10. **Safety**—Young person feels safe at home, at school, and in the neighborhood.
Boundaries and Expectations	11. **Family boundaries**—Family has clear rules and consequences and monitors young people's behavior.
	12. **School boundaries**—School provides clear rules and consequences.
	13. **Neighborhood boundaries**—Neighbors take responsibility for monitoring young people's behavior.
	14. **Adult role models**—Parent(s) and other adults model positive, responsible behavior.
	15. **Positive peer influence**—Young person's best friends model responsible behavior.
	16. **High expectations**—Both parent(s) and teachers encourage the young person to do well.
Constructive	17. **Creative activities**—Young person spends three or more hours per week in lessons or practice in music, theatre or other arts.
	18. **Youth programs**—Young person spends three or more hours per week in sports, clubs, or organizations at school and/or in the community.
	19. **Religious community**—Young person spends one or more hours per week in activities in a religious institution.
	20. **Time at home**—Young person is out with friends "with nothing special to do" two or fewer nights per week.

Forty Developmental Assets (continued)

Search Institute has identified the following building blocks of healthy development that help young people grow up healthy, caring and responsible.

EXTERNAL ASSETS

Category	Asset Name and Definition
Commitment to Learning	21. **Achievement motivation**—Young person is motivated to do well in school.
	22. **School engagement**—Young person is actively engaged in learning.
	23. **Homework**—Young person reports doing at least one hour of homework every school day.
	24. **Bonding at school**—Young person cares about her or his school.
	25. **Reading for pleasure**—Young person reads for pleasure three or more hours per week.
Positive Values	26. **Caring**—Young person places high value on helping other people.
	27. **Equality and social justice**—Young person places high value on promoting equality and reducing hunger and poverty.
	28. **Integrity**—Young person acts on convictions and stands up for her or his beliefs.
	29. **Honesty**—Young person "tells the truth even when it is not easy."
	30. **Responsibility**—Young person accepts and takes personal responsibility.
	31. **Restraint**—Young person believes it is important not to be sexually active or to use alcohol or other drugs.
Social Competencies	32. **Planning and decision-making**—Young person knows how to plan ahead and make choices.
	33. **Interpersonal competence**—Young person has empathy, sensitivity, and friendship skills.
	34. **Cultural competence**—Young person has knowledge of and comfort with people of different cultural, racial or ethnic backgrounds.
	35. **Resistance skills**—Young person can resist negative peer pressure and dangerous situations.
	36. **Peaceful conflict resolution**—Young person seeks to resolve conflict nonviolently.
Positive Identity	37. **Personal power**—Young person feels he or she has control over "things that happen to me."
	38. **Self-esteem**—Young person reports having a high self-esteem.
	39. **Sense of purpose**—Young person reports that "my life has a purpose."
	40. **Positive view of personal future**—Young person is optimistic about her or his personal future.

Note: Based on total national sample of 250,000 public school youth, grades six to twelve. Percentages indicate how many youth engage in each pattern based on the level of the original thirty assets they experience.[6]

From here, the research gets even more interesting. When the Search Institute presented the 30 developmental assets, they were presented with no numeric value attached. In other words, asset number 5 was just as important as asset number 25. Yet Mert believed that one asset might have more value than the others, that one of the assets may have a direct impact on as many as 20 to 25 of the other assets. At the time this book was written, the research was still being conducted to confirm the relationship between this one asset and the other assets, but the early findings have concluded that this one asset is directly linked to at least 25 (out of 40) of the assets. Would you like to know what one asset has the ability to impact 25 of your child's other assets? It is the asset titled Religious Community. And in a personal conversation I had with Mert, he stated that Religious Community had more to do with a personal faith relationship than anything else.

So let me summarize: We want our children to do well and avoid the at-risk behaviors of drugs, alcohol, gangs and promiscuous sexual activity. Search Institute discovered that 25 or more assets greatly increase your child's likelihood of doing well and avoiding at-risk behaviors. A further study has revealed that a personal faith relationship can bring your child 25+ assets. Therefore, if you want your child to avoid the risk of straying into the at-risk behaviors of drugs, alcohol and promiscuous sexual activity, it can be concluded that faith greatly increases the likelihood that your children will do well and not stray into at-risk behaviors.

Yet, in saying this, it must be made clear that even if parents do everything right, their kids may still stray. I have known many God-following, obedient parents who have done everything right at home, but in spite of their best efforts, they have seen their children stray into drugs, alcohol or promiscuous sexual activity. There is, however, another important truth that you must understand: Even if your kids stray, you stay.

In the parable of the lost son in Luke 15:11-32, we find the story of a dad who had, in all likelihood, done everything right in his home regarding faith at home. Yet in spite of this, one of his sons decided to take his inheritance and strayed into the ways of the world. Pastors normally focus on the activity of the wayward son, but I want to draw your attention to the father in this story. What did the father do? Did he abandon the faith because, even though he had done everything right, his son still strayed? Did he give up on God? No, he stayed faithful and committed to his God. Now don't get me wrong. I'm sure he prayed many times a day for his son, but he never wavered from his faith. And later, after his son had hit rock bottom and come home, where was his dad? Right where he had been. Nothing had changed about him or his faith.

So, as we promote and equip people for Faith@Home living, we must be sure to stress that not all parents will have successful children, but the chances of success will be greatly increased. The one thing that we can control is ourselves and our own faith walk. Therefore, even if our kids stray, we are called, as Faith@Home-focused individuals, to stay. This provides a place for our kids to come home to when they need us.

Trap#8: Support of the Senior Pastor Is Necessary

Earlier, I stated how important it is for the senior pastor to buy into Faith@Home if you are going to be a Faith@Home-focused church. Yet in advocating this, I also want to validate the other side of the coin: obtaining the support of the senior pastor is not absolutely essential. You can get started without it. Pastor Dave Teixeira wrote the following on this matter:

> Would it be great if the senior pastor was on board with your vision to empower families to live out the faith in their homes? Yes. Would it be great to have sermons about the importance of investing in our children frequently come from the pulpit of your church? Definitely. And would it be nice to feel like the children, youth and family budget and staffing were a high priority to the leadership of your church? Absolutely. But here's the reality . . . in your church this may or may not happen. And furthermore, you might

not have any control over this. But you can do it anyway. Yes, little old you, the one with the half-office in the back corner of the church basement. I hate to say this, but my coauthor was a senior pastor, and to tell you something you already know, senior pastors can be a bit narcissistic. They think if they don't start it, support it or promote it, it won't happen. I love you, Mark, but that's not always true. [Faith@Home events] are very easily begun with little money and support from the bigwigs of your congregation, including the senior pastor. Now, I'm not saying to do anything in secrecy, or even under the radar of your pastor. However, even without your pastor doing cartwheels, you can begin to move forward. Just let the appropriate people know you are going to start some training events for families and get started. Start small, build a team of people with a similar passion and watch it grow. In a few years, when enough momentum has grown, you had better believe the senior pastor will get on board (and probably take all the credit for your work)![7]

While I take exception to Dave's comment about senior pastors being narcissistic, the rest of what he says is true. This movement can begin without your senior pastor's complete buy-in or support. Or perhaps better stated, you don't need to wait for your senior pastor to get it before you begin making it happen. In fact, don't wait! Make it happen for the sake of the people in your church who are struggling to live for Christ at home. Eventually, your senior pastor will come to understand the importance of Faith@Home.

Trap #9: Faith@Home Isn't for Singles

Another common trap to avoid is the idea that Faith@Home isn't for singles. Where do singles face their greatest temptations? At home, whether that be an apartment, dorm room, condominium or single-family house. Pornography, sexual promiscuity, alcohol and drug abuse are all temptations faced at home. Singles, especially young adults today, need Faith@Home help and they deeply desire a singles or young adult ministry that will help them bring Christ and Christlike living into their lifestyle at home. Ask your singles or young adults if they would rather have another "meat market" type singles event or one that would provide ideas and resources on how to be a more godly single at home, and see what they say.

An easy way to develop a Faith@Home-focused singles or young adult ministry is to simply gather a group of singles or young adults and start by looking at Romans 7:14-24. Then ask them, "What would Faith@Home-focused singles [or young adults] do? What would be things they wouldn't do?" Then design your singles or young adult ministry around events, Bible studies or small groups focused on helping them to do and not do the things they are supposed to do and not do at home.

Trap #10: It's Too Late for Seniors to Get Involved

As I described in chapter 3, there is no such thing as a retirement plan when it comes to Faith@Home. One of the things seniors commonly ask me about is whether it is okay for them to stay engaged in the faith life of their children and/or grandchildren. My response is always the same: "You can stop when Satan stops!" As far as I'm concerned, it is never too late for seniors to practice faith at home, and we need to make sure that they stay in the game spiritually with their children and grandchildren. Faith@Home can be used to reengage your seniors in the battle to bring Christ and Christlike living into the home. So make sure your seniors understand the critical role they are being called to play in your Faith@ Home initiative, or else they will think this is something for families and not for them.

Trap #11: After Several Years, You'll Need Something New

A final trap to avoid will come when you hit years four, five and beyond and feel that you need to move on to something new. We live at a time when a lot of people are constantly looking for the next new thing. We are great at starting things, but we are not so good at maintaining things. Read what Jesus said:

> *If you hold to my teaching*, you are really my disciples. Then you will know the truth, and the truth will set you free (John 8:31-32, emphasis added).

Everyone likes the idea of knowing the truth and being set free by it but Jesus said that we must do something first: "Hold to my teaching." By the time we hit years four or five we will have most of our Faith@Home initiatives in place, and it is in those years and beyond that we will be tempted to move on to the next thing. We must avoid this trap at all costs, because, as stated earlier, reestablishing the home as the primary place for nurturing faith is going to take *at least* one generation.

One of my favorite portions of Scripture is found in John 15. Jesus, having completed His public ministry, had a private, intimate conversation with His disciples before He began His journey to the cross. (The disciples were not aware of this, but we are, so we realize that these were some final words of wisdom and insight that Jesus was imparting to them before He left them.) In the midst of this heartfelt teaching, Jesus repeated one particular word 11 times in 7 verses. It is the only place recorded in Scripture where Jesus repeated Himself this emphatically—and to His most fully devoted followers, no less. What is it that Jesus felt was so important that He repeated it and then kept repeating to make sure they remembered? "Remain." Jesus admonished His disciples to remain in Him. Why did Jesus have to emphasize this point so strongly? Because He knew that they would be tempted to disengage or fall away.

When it comes to practicing faith at home, we too will be tempted to disengage or fall away. There won't be anything new about Faith@Home, so we will be tempted to spend more time or energy on the latest new thing we need to do as a church. When it comes to Faith@Home, we need to avoid the trap of moving on to something else and instead stay ruthlessly committed to remaining with it.

Future Wins

Now that we have identified some of the traps in becoming a Faith@Home-focused church, let's look at some of the future things that are in store for us if we stay the course.

Unity

As a pastor, I was involved in leading multiple movements in the churches I served. I had a chance to be a part of a seeker movement, a small-groups movement, a contemporary worship movement, as well as a missional movement. The one thing I can say about each of these movements is that while each was important and necessary for us as a church, none of these necessarily produced unity. Not everyone likes being seeker focused, and everyone did not get excited about being in small groups. I also discovered that not everyone loves contemporary worship (no real surprise there), and to my surprise and chagrin, everyone didn't buy into the idea of getting more engaged in missional activity as a church.

Yet when I stood before the church and announced that one of the next initiatives we were going to lead was to be a Faith@Home-focused church, which meant that we would leverage every ministry of the church to equip people to live out their faith at home, I received a standing ovation at all three of our services! Seniors came up to me after the service and said, "That sounds great, Pastor. Wish we would have started this 30 years ago." I even had young adults who came up to me and said, "That's something that excites me to hear that we will be doing as a church." The Faith@Home emphasis was something that united us as a church.

Being a former senior pastor, I realize that nothing is harder to achieve than unity in the church. The beauty of the Faith@Home movement is that it is something that everyone can understand, support and buy into. I have yet to have a senior pastor tell me that they launched the Faith@Home movement in their church and it caused a church split. Who is going to stand up and say, "Pastor, I do not think we should be Faith@Home focused!"

Does that mean there won't be resistance? Absolutely not. In fact, you should expect resistance, if for no other reason than the fact that Satan doesn't want this. Satan doesn't want you to be a Faith@Home-focused church, so he is going to do whatever he can to prevent, disrupt and discourage you as you move forward. But that doesn't mean you won't have unity in your church.

Stronger Mission, Vision and Strategy

While every church has mission, vision or strategy that God has called it to fulfill, I truly believe that no matter what a church's current mission, vision or strategy is, it can be even better if you make it more Faith@Home focused. I liken it to being nearsighted. Many people wear glasses or contacts to correct their nearsightedness. They can pretty much only see what is right in front of them without their glasses or contacts, but with their glasses on or contacts in, they can see a lot better and farther. In the same way, I believe that many churches have a mission or vision that they can see, but it's nearsighted or church focused. However, when the church puts on its Faith@Home lenses, it is then able to see its mission, vision or strategy extend all the way into the homes of its people.

A Faith@Home emphasis forces us to ask another layer of questions that we have not been asking, such as:

- How will this ministry event or program impact how our people live out their faith at home?
- What can we do to make this ministry event or program more Faith@Home focused?

For example, if your church's vision is to be a people "of prayer," then when you add the Faith@Home component, it simply becomes a vision in which you want your people to be people "of prayer at home." If you have a missional vision, then you want to help your people live out their mission at home as well as in the community and world. If your vision is discipleship, then you want to help your people live out and nurture discipleship in the home. Do you see how Faith@Home makes your vision stronger?

Instantaneous Impact

While I have discussed the importance of making a long-term commitment to Faith@Home, there are some short-term or immediate things that you can anticipate seeing. Pastor Jim Toohey, Faith@ Home pastor at Promontory Community Church in British Columbia, Canada, recently shared this list of "14 Wins" with actual testimonies he has received since launching a Faith@Home initiative in his church just two years earlier:

1. Parents realize they can do this without being an expert and that God indeed blesses their efforts.

   > "The boys have loved it. They want more and more stories. It's been awesome to chat with them about God and try to answer their questions. I can do this!"

2. Children asking their parents how they can ask Jesus into their hearts.

3. Parents being the ones to lead their own children to Christ. Now there's a moment you wouldn't trade for the world!

   > "Our youngest, Jake, asked how he can get Jesus in his heart. I asked if he believed in God and if he believed that Jesus is God's son. Jake and my oldest son, Cal, both said yes, so I asked them if they would like to say a prayer to invite God into their heart and both my boys said yes!"

4. Parents describing how deep and meaningful their conversations have become with their kids with both chil-

dren and parents sharing things about their lives and hearts that they would not have except for the fact that they were doing a simple Christ-centered activity . . . in the home.

> "Jim, it is great! Both of our children enjoy the story. We all love it and are having great family discussions! Thank you so much!"

> "The kids love their new Bible. We've been reading it at dinner time and tonight we read about John baptizing Jesus and I asked them if they remembered what being baptized means. I told them that you've invited Jesus into your heart."

> "It's so wonderful to see them asking questions and wanting to read the Bible."

5. Both parents and kids growing in their faith because of what's happening in the home.

> "I find my knowledge of the Bible has expanded immensely and I'm able to pull references from these resources much more freely without feeling weird or uncomfortable."

6. Children have sleepovers or friends over for dinner and still want their parents to have devotions or read the bible to them . . . because it's really cool and fun.

7. The neighbors' kids going home and asking their parents if they would do devotions or read the Bible to them.

> "When your neighbors come over to find out more about your faith because of the difference they see in your family, and how surprised they

were to discover their children are really interested about God and faith (while you try to hide how surprised you are that your neighbors would be interested about God and faith)."

8. Children nagging their parents to do devotions, prayer or Bible readings.

"Mostly our challenge as parents to actually do the stuff with our kids, not that the kids have any problems wanting to do it; in fact, they will bug us if we don't."

"When we miss a few nights, Madison is really encouraging us to catch up on the missed ones."

9. Achieving the wow factor for parents in your Take It Home events.

"Wow, that's so simple; I can do that!"

10. Realizing that your family had an unscheduled conversation about God and faith for a period of time that you almost didn't notice because it felt as natural and effortless as breathing.

"We talk so much more now about Jesus. I even hear my husband talking to the girls about what we've discussed and it is just amazing!"

11. Listening to your kids come home from school and tell you how they applied God's Word to their words and actions and the difference it made.

12. Kids holding their parents accountable to truths they are learning as a family. Mom and Dad being humble enough to receive it.

13. As a pastor, being a part of helping people begin their spiritual journey as a family.

> "Thanks again for all you do. You hold a special place in our hearts as I truly believe you gave us that little nudge we needed to begin our spiritual journey as a family."

> "Thank you for connecting with the families and equipping us with tools to raise our kids in a house full of faith. We feel that our family has grown in many ways, even if the changes are small and slow."

14. A year after a particular event, having a family give a testimonial about how much God has made a difference in their home simply using the resource they were given and putting it into practice. (And your wow factor having just grown exponentially by their testimony!)

You can expect to see similar wins in the early years of your Faith@Home movement.

Multigenerational Impact

Probably one of the most exciting aspects of the Faith@Home movement is the multigenerational impact it has. Through the Faith@Home movement, we get to be a part of something that is going to outlive us! I don't know about you, but that excites me. And it's definitely better than any building program, because we are building something that is going to positively impact the faith lives of generations of followers. We are going to see the fruit of our labors when we are in heaven. Parents will bless, pray, worship, serve and read the Bible in the home with their kids, and all because you decided to become a Faith@Home-focused church three generations earlier for their great-grandparents!

So, why should you want to become a Faith@Home-focused church? Why should you want to equip the home to be the primary place where faith is lived and nurtured? Deuteronomy 6:2 tells us why: "So that you, your children and their children after them may fear the Lord your God as long as you live by keeping all his decrees and commands that I give you, and so that you may enjoy long life." Faith@Home is about helping people today follow God and His ways in an authentic, 24/7 way so that they, their children and children's children will enjoy everlasting life.

Ponder, Pray and Discuss

1. Have you been ensnared by any of the traps? Which one(s)? Why?

2. How can you become disentangled from the trap(s) you're in? What concrete ideas can help you move forward?

3. Do you think that the wins, or benefits, of becoming a Faith@Home-focused church are worth the changes you have to make to your current way of doing church?

4. Besides the wins discussed here, what other wins do you imagine are possible for your congregation? For the Church as a whole?

CHAPTER SUMMARY

- Dot 1: A Faith@Home-driven church starts with the pastor's personal commitment.

- Dot 2: The leaders of your church need to be as committed as you are.

- Dot 3: Commitment to the movement must be long-term.

- Dot 4: The leadership in your church needs to be engaged in your Faith@Home movement.

- Dot 5: Passion for Faith@Home must be ignited and fanned in the church body.

- Dot 6: Maintenance of the Faith@Home focus is essential to success.

- Testimonials prove that Faith@Home works.

- Ongoing support is available in a variety of ways for and from many different people.

- A prayer and a blessing for all who read this book.

6

How Do We Connect the Dots and Keep Going?

The entire faith-at-home movement is not about programs, numbers or facilities. It's about Jesus. Nothing more. Nothing less.
DICK HARDEL

ANOTHER VOICE SAYS...

From Focus on the Family Canada

Wow! About three and a half thousand years ago the idea of faith at home was first written down on papyrus. It was the word from God to Moses and His people, and it was a repetition of the Law. Here we are in the early part of the twenty-first century and rediscovering God's timeless plan. How crazy is that?! We at Focus on the Family Canada are profoundly humbled by God's call and the timeless opportunity to build faith at home. We are calling homes and churches to revisit the command to pass on the things of God "when you sit at home and when you walk along the road, when you lie down and when you get up" [Deut. 6:7]. The concept is so simple and yet so profound. And as each movement of God throughout history, He raises up those who will be His mouthpiece and messengers. We believe Mark Holmen is such a person. In the days ahead, we anticipate moving accounts of how households have returned to God's timeless plan as a result of the obedient efforts of a guy like Mark, and we are thrilled to partner with him in this initiative. Get ready for Faith@Home. Let's go, Mark, and see what God's got in store!

Remember connect-the-dot worksheets? When I was a child, I loved connecting the dots. I found something almost magical about how a page of dots could slowly form into a clear image as I methodically connected the dots in order. I loved connect-the-dots so much that sometimes I would take a plain sheet of paper and randomly place dots all over the page. Then I would start connecting the dots to see if an image formed on its own. Obviously, this wasn't as successful as preprinted worksheets. But either way, I found myself entertained and enthralled by connecting dots.

Often, when I attend a conference, sit down with an innovative leader or read a book full of ideas and concepts, I inwardly find myself saying, *Would someone please connect the dots for me?* I love random thinkers, but only for so long! Eventually, I need time to process what they're saying so that I can connect their ideas to my reality.

This was usually the case whenever I sat down with Dr. Dick Hardel, director of the Youth and Family Institute. He could put a thousand Faith@Home dots on the wall in less than 30 minutes, but he never connected them! Usually, he just looked at me and said, "That's your job. Have fun!" To be perfectly honest, that's why we made a good team—he loved to throw dots on the wall, and I loved connecting them.

So in this final chapter, I want to help you connect the dots for leading a faith at home movement in your church. Just to be upfront, even after we've connected the dots, the image will still be a very big picture without a lot of detail. You'll need to add that yourself, because no two churches are the same. However, we can connect the dots and provide a basic outline that you can then customize for your own ministry.

So let's get started connecting dots!

Dot 1: Make a Personal Commitment

The journey to becoming a Faith@Home-driven church begins with you, the pastor. God has called you to serve your congregation and to lead it faithfully. Every day, I'm humbled that God chose me to be a pastor and missionary to the Faith@Home movement, because I know that I'm not qualified to do so. I'm in full agreement with the apostle Paul when he wrote, "I am less than the least." I'm a work in progress, and each day seems like another day of training and growth.

I don't know how you ended up with this book in your hands, but God does. Somehow, God placed this book in your hands "for such a time as this." Be assured that he did so for a reason, because that's simply how God works. With Him, there are no accidents or coincidences. He has a plan and purpose for you as a leader, and He'll use books, conferences and other leaders to influence you in the direction He wants to take and grow you.

As a pastor, perhaps you didn't realize the grave situation that exists when it comes to how people live out their faith at home. If so, that's okay, because now you do. The good news is that you can do something about it! You can start by putting on a permanent set of Faith@Home lenses that will color—in a positive way—the way you lead your church. With this new set of lenses in place, you'll learn to base success less on numbers, programs and buildings and more on bringing Christ and Christlike living into the home. You'll remember that Jesus was, is and always will be the answer every person and family needs to succeed. Unfortunately, Jesus has been standing outside the home for too long. It's time for us as pastors to help usher Him into the center of every family again.

There's a great painting by Raphael titled *Jesus at the Door*. It depicts Jesus standing at a door, knocking. A vine winds around the doorway, making it appear that the door hasn't been opened for some time. I've heard that when Raphael first showed the painting, a critic pointed out that the artist had forgotten to paint a handle on the door. The painter simply replied, "I didn't forget, the handle is on the other side of the door."

We have a God who stands at the door of our homes knocking. He has always been there, and He will wait there until we let Him in: "Here I am! I stand at the door and knock. If anyone hears my voice and opens the door, I will come in and eat with him, and he with me" (Rev. 3:20).

The Faith@Home movement begins when we as pastors understand that our role is to help usher Jesus into the center of people's hearts and homes. As Dr. Dick Hardel shared with me, "The entire Faith@Home movement is not about programs, numbers or facilities. It's about Jesus. Nothing more. Nothing less."

Where are our eyes as pastors? Are they on the building across town that we wish we had? Are they on the latest and greatest program we wish we could implement in our churches? Are they on the worship leader we wish we could hire? Or are they on Jesus, who stands at the door of every home knocking . . . knocking . . . knocking. He patiently waits for someone to hear Him and open the door so that He can come in and transform that person's and that family's life.

Are you helping the people God has given you to hear Him knocking and to open the door for Him to come in? That's our primary focus. Nothing more. Nothing less.

Dot 2: Bring Church Leadership on Board

Now that you've put on a set of Faith@Home lenses, the next dot that needs to be connected is to the leadership of your church. The leaders of your church need to become as committed to the faith at home movement as you are. They need to understand the crisis that families are in, recognize the need to bring Christ and Christlike living into the home, and embrace the changes that need to be made to become a Faith@Home-focused church.

Frankly, one of the mistakes I made during my first years at Ventura Missionary Church was to not take the time to help bring the leaders of the church to the place where I was. I understood the reality and the need when it came to families, had a huge sense of urgency driving me, and recognized what we needed to do to become a Faith@Home-focused church. But I didn't take the time to make sure the church's leaders saw the need and vision as clearly as I did.

My hope and prayer for you is that with the help of this book and the other resources I've recommended, you'll be able to help the leaders of your church have the same focus that you have. Take time to bring them on board. Don't shortcut it, because some big leadership decisions lie ahead, and the leaders need to be united with you in this.

Dot 3: Make Your Commitment Long-term

You can't change your church overnight, so you must make a long-term commitment to becoming a Faith@Home-focused church. You and your leaders can only establish this long-term commitment if you intentionally do three things that I mentioned in chapter 4:

1. Weave the Faith@Home commitment into your mission, vision and strategy as a church.
2. Begin devoting funds to provide the resources necessary for the movement.
3. Empower someone to be your Faith@Home champion who will work with every ministry of the church to help them equip the home to be the primary place where faith is nurtured.

When I look at that list, I realize that none of these steps looks quick or easy. That's another reason why it's so important to have the leadership of your church on board.

Weaving Faith@Home language into your mission, vision and strategy might be relatively easy, or it might mean you need to do some significant reworking. In some cases, the mission, vision and strategy of a church had been established for years and the idea of changing it in any way is a scary proposition. If that's true in your church, ask yourself and leaders of the church if your mission, vision and strategy truly address the Faith@Home crisis facing families today. Again, you probably don't need to throw out everything you are currently doing. You might just need to tweak things a little to make your mission, vision and strategy even better!

Raising the initial funds and growing your budget to support your Faith@Home movement over the long haul will also take leadership. You probably don't have funds in your budget to start providing resources to every family in your church in order to equip them to be faith nurturers in their own homes. So I encourage you to devote a Sunday to making a faith at home appeal in which you focus on many of the points we've covered in this book:

- The reality that Christlike living is not happening in homes today
- The role that the Church has played in enabling this to happen
- How you intend to reclaim homes for Christ through a comprehensive faith at home strategy (give examples of the type of resources you want to provide for Take It Home events)
- The need for this to happen

Once you have cast the faith at home vision, make the appeal to your congregation and set a big goal! Then give people an opportunity to respond to everything you have said. If all goes well, this kind of Faith@Home appeal will provide the start-up resources you need to launch the movement. Keep in mind that you'll still need to fund your Faith@Home movement on a permanent basis through your annual budget. Hopefully, the Faith@Home appeal will give you a couple of years until the church budget can support the movement on an ongoing basis.

Finding the right staff person or volunteer to provide oversight and leadership to the Faith@Home movement in your church can also take time. You might discover that the right person is already on your staff and all you need to do is simply rework a job description to give that individual the authority needed to lead the movement. Or you might find that you need to make some difficult decisions in order to staff this movement appropriately. I can't stress enough the importance of finding the *right* person to lead this movement in your church.

John Maxwell, who some call America's expert on leadership, boldly proclaims, "Everything rises and falls on leadership."[1] Just a few simple words, but vital advice. So I urge you to invest in the person who will lead this movement in your church. You probably won't find someone with a lot of experience, because we're at the very beginning of this new movement that God is leading. So look for a person who has the heart, passion and gifts to lead. (For help with this, see the children, youth and family ministry pastor job description in appendix 2.) Then invest in this leader by sending him or her to training events and conferences to meet with like-minded people leading the movement in other churches.

Choosing the leader for the Faith@Home movement in your church is so critical that you might need to make some difficult decisions in order to put the right person in place who can lead the movement forward successfully. For example, when we made Faith@ Home one of VMC's top priorities, our church had a preschool, a K to 8 school, a children's ministry and a youth ministry. Each of these ministries operated in its own silo, and the leaders had never been pulled together to think or work as a team. We knew that becoming a faith at home-driven church meant that we needed to hire a pastor to oversee this team and drive the movement.

Unfortunately, in order to accommodate this new leader, we had to eliminate another pastoral position. One of the hardest days I've ever had as a pastor was the day I had to tell a very committed and caring pastor who had served VMC faithfully for more than 15 years that his position was being eliminated. To this day, I'll never forget his gracious response: "As hard as it is to hear this, I want you to know that I think you made the right decision." In the months that followed, God provided for this pastor to continue to serve and use his gifts in a church in a neighboring community. Although this decision was difficult, it was the right decision for the long-term future of VMC and the commitment we had made.

I would like to say that everything was rosy after that. However, after we hired our youth and family ministry pastor, we discovered that people on our team didn't share our Faith@Home commitment. We had to make more changes—which weren't any easier. In fact, it took almost three years to get to the place where the church had a united Faith@Home-focused youth and family ministry team.

Fast-forward 10 years to when I announced that I was resigning as the senior pastor of Ventura Missionary church to become a full-time missionary to the Faith@Home movement. Six weeks after I completed my service to VMC, Pastor Dave Teixeira, the church's youth and family ministry pastor and my co-Faith@Home champion at VMC, was called to be their next senior pastor! Faith@Home was so engrained into the church culture that they didn't want to move away from it. Even better, Dave no longer needs to hire a Faith@Home champion to fill his position, because Faith@Home is woven into every ministry and each ministry leader now has a Faith@Home heartbeat.

While becoming a Faith@Home-focused church begins with you as the pastor, it will require you and the church's leadership to make some decisions that will prove that this commitment is real and long term. If you make the changes I've described, your church will remain a Faith@Home-focused church whether you stay there or not.

As pastors, we need to take the passion we have to see Christ in the center of every home and transfer it into the very DNA of the church. This takes time and fortitude. However, the hard work you put in now to become a Faith@Home-focused church will keep your church on the right course for generations to come! Even if transferring your Faith@Home commitment takes a few years, it will all be worth it. Remember, "Religious life in the home is more influential than the Church."

Dot 4: Foster Extended Leadership's Buy-In

The next dot that needs to be connected is for the extended leadership of your church to engage in your Faith@Home movement. The Faith at Home Leadership Summit outline in appendix 3 can help you foster buy-in from the leaders of all the ministries of your church.

I'll never forget the first Leadership Summit that Dave Teixeira and I led at VMC. To be honest, it was the first time all the leaders of the ministries of the church—including the leaders of our men's, women's, children's, youth, adult, small groups, missions, and other ministries—had ever met in the same room together. Dave and I shared with them some basic statistics about the state of families, including the reality that less than 10 percent of the families in most churches truly have Christ and Christlike living in the center of their homes. We also gave a very abstract vision for how we could become a Faith@Home-focused church. Then we asked what they thought.

The response was overwhelming! Each leader shared how faith at home was the primary stumbling block he or she was facing. The idea of coming together to work collaboratively on the problem was something each of them couldn't wait to start. We began laying out our Take It Home events. When the meeting concluded, we had a plan to launch eight Take It Home events in the first year and to add five more the following year.

Even more important than this plan was the infectious and contagious spirit that developed among the leadership of the church. We all saw where we were heading and understood the role we would play in helping to make our congregation a Faith@Home-focused church. In following years, the summit became a time to share success stories, hear testimonies of lives that had been changed, review and revise the plans for the upcoming year, and share ideas for the future. From that first leadership summit meeting on, we moved from being a church *with* a family ministry to being a Faith@Home-focused church.

The logo you see on the previous page grew out of one of our Faith@Home Leadership Summits. Our children, youth and family team created it to represent VMC's Faith@Home movement. This logo appeared on literature sent out from our children, youth and family ministries. I also used the logo in our new-member classes and with visitors to describe our commitment to be a Faith@Home-focused church. (Feel free to use this logo or create something yourself to represent the commitment your church is making to focus on Faith@Home.)

Dot 5: Stir Passion in the Church Body

Another dot you'll need to connect pertains to the people who faithfully attend and serve your church body. Over time, a church takes on the passion and personality of its leader. The people of your church will become passionate about what you're passionate about. As you become a Faith@Home-focused pastor, you will need to stir the same passion in your church.

One way to share your outlook is through a sermon series. As I mentioned earlier, one sermon series a year isn't enough to keep the Faith@Home movement alive in a church. However, one sermon series is definitely enough to launch the movement and create a sense of urgency and expectancy in your congregation. In *Take It Home: Inspiration and Events to Help Parents Spiritually Transform Their Children*, Dave Teixeira and I outline a five-week sermon series that can serve as a good movement launcher for congregations.[2] Such a sermon series will give your congregation the opportunity to see your passion and commitment. It can start the Faith@Home ball rolling and give the movement a push that will continue gaining momentum for years to come. (One word of caution: Be careful not to preach this kind of sermon series before you're ready to launch the movement, because people will be ready to respond. Remember, even if they're not aware of it, they've been waiting a long time for something like this!)

Another way to engage your congregation is to spotlight the Take It Home events you've started. Keep your congregation aware of what your church is doing to bring Christ and Christlike living into the home. Show the resources you give away at each Take It Home event. This allows the people of your church to see how families are using the resources they've been providing.

In one church where I spoke as a guest, the pastor placed a faith chest on the stage and slowly filled it with all the resources the church would provide through their Take It Home events during the year. The pastor explained each resource and how it would help the family in the home. When he was finished, he thanked the church for its Faith@Home commitment and for the funds they had provided to help make Take It Home events happen. This visual illustration conveyed to the people just how serious the church was about equipping the home to be the primary place where faith is nurtured. As the pastor finished, I remembered thinking, *I'm going to do that in my church!*

Dot 6: Maintain Momentum

The final dot you need to connect is the "maintaining the momentum" dot. As with any new movement, the leaders and members of your church will have a lot of passion and excitement in the beginning. But over time, their attention and focus might wander and they might lose some of their commitment and drive.

Remember that a Faith@Home focus requires a long-term commitment. Your church must stay the course for the next 20 to 30 years and beyond! While programs might have life cycles, this isn't just another program. Here are a few suggestions for how you can keep the Faith@Home ball rolling.

First, at a leadership level, make sure that your evaluation of both paid and volunteer leaders includes the impact that their ministry is having on your church's Faith@Home movement. How is their ministry helping instill Faith@Home? How are the people they minister to becoming more Faith@Home driven? What influence has their ministry had on Faith@Home? When your ministry leaders realize that Faith@Home is part of how their job performance will be evaluated, they'll be sure to focus their attention on the home instead of what happens at church. Another way to keep the movement moving is to continually add and strengthen Take It Home events. The Take It Home strategy you implement will continue to evolve and get better over time. Pastor Dave Teixeira describes it this way:

What just happened? I thought as I left church one morning. I never thought I would get my rear whooped by a bunch of two-year-olds, but I just had. It was our first Take It Home event for twos and their parents on family blessings. We had a great morning planned—food, music, a puppet show and even a little set portraying a child's bedroom where we would show parents what blessing your child each night before bed might look like.

Feeling like the parents would want some Bible exposition on the theology behind blessing, I had come prepared with about 10 minutes of teaching on the subject. Then we would get practical and begin helping parents write and practice blessing their own children. For some reason (and this is surprising, because at the time I had a two-year-old) in my mind the two-year-olds were going to sit quietly in Mommy or Daddy's laps while I talked peacefully with the parents about the history and theology of blessing. You know what happened instead? Kids were everywhere! Moms were up and chasing, Dads were frustrated and I literally could not get through one sentence without a major interruption. I felt like we had failed.

But here's the point. We hadn't failed! First of all, several parents from that group told me later that they had begun blessing their children and one father told me that his daughter won't go to sleep without his blessing her first. (Again, the goal isn't how well the event goes!) Second, and most importantly, we had learned. Following the event we went right to work evaluating and brainstorming how we might change the format for next time to help things run smoother. And you know what, things DID run smoother!

This year we tried our first Computer Savvy Parents Take It Home event for parents of middle school and high school students. It was OK. Honestly, I gave the event a D+ (I'm a hard grader). However, I promise you that next year's event will be better because we learned so much this first time. During the question-and-answer time we learned what kinds of questions parents will ask. Watching parents and kids interact, we discovered where the tension points between parents and kids lie. We found out how much time it takes to do a virtual tour of the Internet and what parents want most in terms of filtering info. So, despite our D+ this year, the event was a success and a step in the right direction. Next year I'm anticipating at least a B.[3]

I love what the Faith@Home team at VMC came up with for Take It Home events. The resources they found and the events they provided continually amazed me. My own family was blessed through the Take It Home events that we had the opportunity to participate in. Each year, the church adds a few more. The events they continue to offer seem to get stronger each year. The members of this team have a long-term vision and commitment! They recognize that these Take It Home events aren't something the church does for a season but that they make up a permanent part of how they do ministry to children and youth and whole families. The team is continually looking for ways to improve its Take It Home strategy, and they consistently look at resources, visit other churches and attend conferences. As a result, the Faith@Home focus gets stronger and better each year.

That leads to the final way you can maintain momentum: Affirm positive behavior. When you see or hear how a ministry has made a Faith@Home shift, no matter how subtle it may be, affirm that change! Nothing means more to paid staff and volunteers than hearing an affirming word from the pastor. Because the move to becoming a faith at home-driven church is a gradual process, you'll need to gently support your leaders.

Will there be failures and misses? Absolutely. I could fill at least another chapter with all the mistakes and misses I've had through the years. But at least we were trying, and in every situation we learned something that made us better the next time around. Even when your leaders attempt something and fail, affirm them for trying. Not every attempt will succeed, and that can kill momentum unless you affirm the attempt. Often, that's all a leader needs to keep on going.

Will This Really Work?

Throughout this book, I've told many stories about myself and the churches where I've served. I've shared how we implemented a vision, mission and strategy to bring Christ and Christlike living back into the home. I've stuck my neck on the line a bit to tell you about my own experiences, because when it comes to the Faith@ Home movement, I believe that the messenger is the message. I've tried to give you a glimpse of how God has used and blessed me by allowing me to be at the leading edge of this important movement.

Of course, you might be thinking, *Sure, the faith at home way of ministry has worked for you, Mark, because you've helped lead it. But I don't see how it could work in my church.* Before you dismiss it all, I would like to share with you some testimonies from other church leaders who have made a shift to being Faith@Home focused and the impact that this decision had had.

Annette Tarin
Director of Children's Ministry, First Presbyterian Church
and Radiant, Oxnard, California

As Director of Children's Ministry, I work hard to provide effective programming to reach kids for Christ. When I read *Building Faith at Home,* it opened my eyes to the fact that no matter how great a children's program is, it will only be as effective as what happens in the home. I spent my first year in my current ministry trying to carry out my vision by providing a great curriculum that would teach kids God's Word and bring them closer to a personal relationship with Jesus, trained up an awesome children's team and created a loving environment. I realized something was still missing—parents were not carrying out their faith at home. They were not being equipped to understand how important it is to pray with their children, read the Bible together and do devotions. I needed to shift gears; I put on, as Mark Holmen says, "a new set of lenses." I have decided to be more Faith@Home focused in my ministry instead of just trying to reach children. I believe as the parents grow in their role as the spiritual influence in their children's lives, our ministry and our church will be strengthened.

Tim Coltvet
Youth and Family Ministry Pastor, Mount Olivet Lutheran,
Plymouth, Minnesota

As we begin to prepare for the coming year, our church has become increasingly convinced that we need to identify faith in the home as a core strategic principle.

This past January, we decided to invite Mom and Dad to the church building for our junior-high program nights. We were pleased to have Mark Holmen as guest speaker for one of these events. With the sanctuary full of junior-high students and parents, he laid the foundation for a meaningful conversation with our families. He began the journey by asking us a question: "What would it look like for your family to have an extreme home makeover . . . with Christ at the center?"

After this event, our church began to ask volumes of questions and to carry on hours of discussion about our congregation's ability to ensure that future generations would carry with them and pass on faith in Jesus Christ. As we continued the discussion, we slowly realized that this concept was becoming a part of the DNA of our congregation. By the end of our January session, our senior pastor was so moved by the data and critical nature of the discussion that he urged the church council, staff and congregation to help envision and continually embrace a "faith in the home" philosophy in our congregational life.

Exactly what's being born within our congregation, I can't be sure. But it's clear to me that the Holy Spirit is working to redefine the way we pass on the faith in the twenty-first century. Shame on me, as a pastor, for thinking that my sermons on Sunday morning should be the primary arena for faith formation and growth in a young person's life. Now we know from research that a simple question from Mom or Dad like "Where did you meet God today?" will have a much more profound effect on the faith formation of that child.

In the words of another friend of mine, "It's time to alter the home with a home altar." We're completely on board with this vision, and we're seeing our families come to life as they embrace their critical callings for God's kingdom.

Gary Strudler
Children's Pastor, Rolling Hills Community Church
Portland, Oregon

Our Home Court Advantage classes with parents and kids are going extraordinarily well. Parents and kids have been excited to get the one-on-one attention and for parents to walk away with some practical helps and resources to help them be the spiritual leaders they desire to be. We made the jump from three classes last year to providing an event for each grade level this year! Thanks, Mark, for allowing the Lord to use you to speak to people like me! Faith at home was exactly the direction our church wanted and needed to go. It's also amazing that I've been able to share it with other children's leaders in our area.

Lynn Adams
Former Administrative Pastor, Lighthouse Missionary Church
Elkton, Michigan

In 2005, I was introduced to George Barna's book *Transforming Children into Spiritual Champions*. Through that book, God gave me two major visions for ministry. First, we must stop running programs and become deliberate about making disciples who make disciples. Second, we must help parents own the responsibility of training up their own children to be disciples, with the help and support of the church. At that time I really thought it would be a hard sell to parents, but I started sharing the vision personally and publicly.

In answer to prayer, God raised up a team of ten people—including our senior pastor—to attend the Healthy Home Initiative seminar, where many heard Mark Holmen share his Faith@Home vision.

After the seminar, I called together those who had attended. My purpose was twofold: to find out what they had learned, and to come up with some goals to work toward in our local church. They were very enthusiastic and some wanted to start Take It Home events at every age level within the year. In reality, things have moved a little more slowly than that. This team, with a few others, formed a new Family Ministries Council and has met every month since that time.

Our senior pastor, other members of the council, and I have all shared during church services the truth that training up children to be disciples needs to be our top priority. We started a family newsletter, which introduces two family units each month in order to help families get to know one another and also highlights a specific book or resource that parents have found helpful in training up their children. The team also divided the church families into seven groups, with each couple on the team committed to praying faithfully for the spiritual health of families in their group over the course of the month.

We also developed a master schedule that lists the Take It Home events we'll introduce over the course of the next three years. In the meantime, we've paired up multiple age levels so that more families can participate sooner.

I'd like to take this opportunity to thank Mark Holmen for being faithful to share the burden God has laid on his heart. It has certainly changed the way I look at ministry, and the way we do things at Lighthouse Missionary Church.

Jean Perdu
Children's Pastor, Oakridge Presbyterian Church
London, Ontario, Canada

Mark Holmen's main sessions and breakouts on Faith@ Home ministry at the Navigating New Waters: Children's and Family Ministries Conference brought walloping confirmation to the thoughts and prayers of our team. He put into words what we'd been grasping for and gave us spiritual foundations and practical ideas for putting those thoughts into action. We left knowing that God had some new plans for us, but we also left feeling like we'd been trying to take a drink from a fire hydrant!

Not wanting to lose a single drop, our team quickly focused in on the Key Learning from each session. We reviewed our materials and began to plan. Knowing it wasn't possible to implement everything, we focused on small changes that would make a big difference. Our team prayed and planned and launched our Family Zone: Building Faith in Families ministry.

We desire to see children grow to be adults who "Love the Lord their God with all their heart, soul, and mind and to love their neighbors as themselves." We've made it our goal to equip, empower and encourage families to grow in their faith and pass it on to the next generation. A group of woodworking men has become involved and have been building Faith Chests for each child, which parents receive when their infants are baptized. The chests are meant to hold a child's spiritual keepsakes, as well as the resources they'll use to cut their spiritual teeth on. The idea is for each child to have a chest filled with Faith Building tools to pass on to their own family.

We also implemented Faith Builder workshops this year for three of our age groups with more in store for next year. These workshops take place during Sunday service times and parents attend with their children. Each workshop focuses on a specific Faith Tool and provides children and parents with teaching, application and resources to continue honing that Faith Tool in their daily lives.

We're thrilled to see all that God has done with our new Faith@Home focus in less than a year. From this impact, our congregation has a nearly audible buzz that continues to grow as we eagerly anticipate what God will do next!

Ron Brenning
Family Pastor, Grace Chapel
Englewood, Colorado

Can you imagine being a trailblazer for uniting church and home in the twenty-first century? When I met Mark Holmen at his church in Ventura, California, he had the stories to tell and the battle scars of a paradigm change he was working on to return the primary responsibility of parenting back to the parent and challenging the Church to equip them. Uniting these two institutions was no easy path to forge.

I am presently a family pastor in the Denver area and the Faith@Home movement is alive and well at Grace Chapel. The influence has been a result of the insights learned in Mark Holmen's book. We are presently implementing the Take It Home events in our parenting training. We are using the "at home" statement in our messages and teaching. Every parent is aware of the family blessing and they have their own unique story about it. We use the phrase "take it homework" all the time. Our youth group has met with parents before their teenagers get back from a retreat. They were informed on how to engage with their teens at home. This idea came from the Faith@Home movement. The list goes on.

I cannot underestimate the wisdom and insights this paradigm change brings to bridging the gap between church and home. It is biblical, practical and simple to apply. God's hand is certainly upon it.

So Now What?

Welcome to the Faith@Home movement! A burden God placed on my heart when I followed His call to become a full-time missionary to the Faith@Home movement was to be able to serve church leaders after they have either read this book or attended a Faith@Home church seminar. I don't want the Faith@Home movement or message to be seen as a splash-and-dash thing where we simply bring the Faith@Home methodology to you and then move on to the next city, and you're left to your own devices. So let me briefly share a few things that you can tap into for ongoing support if you desire it.

Website
www.faithathome.com

Our website serves as a home base for the Faith@Home movement. It provides ideas, resource recommendations and new insights for church leaders (senior pastors, youth pastors, children's ministry leaders and adult ministry leaders) and households (moms, dads, grandparents, singles and married couples). You will be able to register your church for free as a Faith@Home-focused church; and in doing so, you will be able to see if there are other nearby churches that are implementing Faith@Home strategies. Also at our website you will find ideas and resources from other Faith@Home practitioners from literally all over the world! For example, when I was asked to speak at Beaverton Foursquare Church in Portland, Oregon, they had created a beautiful 12-page full-color brochure that did an incredible job of explaining what the Faith@Home movement/initiative was all about. That brochure is now available at our website for you to view, customize and use in your church. As a pastor, I loved stuff like this because it made our church look good without our having to go through all the time and expense of creating something ourselves! My prayer is that the Faith@Home website will be a valuable place for you to access ideas, resources and partners to aid you as you begin to implement Faith@Home practices in your church.

YouTube
www.youtube.com/user/FaithatHome

Many churches create video clips to promote, inspire or motivate people to become Faith@Home focused. Our YouTube channel has been created so that you can access these video clips for free! The only thing I ask is that you submit at least some of your own video clips to us when you create them in the future, so we can add yours as well. Again, our heartbeat is to steward the things God has given us, not own them.

Twitter
http://twitter.com/MarkHolmen

Using Twitter, you can follow what God is doing in and through the Faith@Home movement. I use Twitter to announce things that God brings me face to face with as I travel across the world for the Faith@Home movement.

Online Coaching for Church Leaders
http://www.faithathome.com/coaching/church-leader-coaching/

One of the exciting doors that God has opened for me is to be able to offer online coaching for church leaders. Each year from

September through May, I provide monthly online coaching for senior pastors, children's ministry leaders and youth leaders. Each coaching session is one hour long and provides not only a hot topic but also a guest practitioner who will join me to give ideas and insights from another perspective. Each coaching session is interactive, meaning you have the ability to ask questions and receive an answer immediately from either myself or my guest. At this web address, you can find more information about the online coaching for church leaders, including a list of topics and guest practitioners I have scheduled for the upcoming year. I have to let you know that there is a fee for online coaching, and let me briefly explain why. As a missionary I am now in a position where I need to raise my own support. My prayer is that you will see the fee for online coaching as a gift you are giving to your Faith@Home missionary as I provide you with ongoing support and encouragement.

Online Coaching for Parents
http://www.faithathome.com/coaching/
parent-coaching/

In the same way that online coaching for church leaders is offered, Faith@Home coaching for moms and dads is also offered. A few years ago, God brought me together with Timothy Smith, M.A., of ParentsCoach.org. Tim Smith, a former children's pastor with a huge Faith@Home heartbeat, felt called by God to leave children's ministry to become a full-time missionary and coach to parents. Tim has written over 17 books and other resources for parents, and he is an incredibly gifted communicator who I believe God has raised up "for such a time as this" to coach parents on how to be Faith@Home-focused moms and dads. Tim lives only 20 minutes away from where I live (another God thing), which opened a door for Faith@Home to provide parent coaching from a nationally recognized parents' coach. Using the address above, you will be able to find out more information about the online coaching available for parents, including topics, age groups and cost information. Why is there a fee? Because like myself, Tim is a full-time missionary who has to raise his own support. So our prayer is that parents will see this fee as a gift to a missionary who is helping them become Faith@Home-focused parents.

A Hope and a Prayer

I sincerely hope and pray that you have come to realize that this isn't a book I simply wrote for you to read and then put on a shelf. My prayer is that you now can understand and better see that God is leading a Faith@Home movement that is spreading all over the world, and that it is a movement you should be a part of. God is clearly on the move to reclaim every household where Satan has positioned himself, and God is using His Bride to bring Christ and Christlike living back into the center of every home.

As I have mentioned throughout this book, I am not the leader of this movement; God is. Therefore, do not give me any credit whatsoever for this movement and do not attach my name as the leader of this movement. Give God all the glory and praise for what He has done with Faith@Home, for it is God and God alone who deserves all the glory and praise.

Yet in saying this, I do humbly believe that God has called me to be a missionary to serve you and this movement. My prayer is that this book will be the beginning of our journey together. You now have a new set of Faith@Home lenses that will give you a new perspective and view on how you lead your ministry and equip the home to be the primary place where faith is lived. I can't wait to see how this new Faith@Home perspective will impact your ministry—and your congregation—in the days, weeks, months and years ahead. Please know that I'm here as *your* missionary to support you, encourage you, be a resource for you and help you in any way that I can.

Let me close with this prayer of blessing from Numbers 6:24-26:

May the Lord continue to bless you and keep you. May the Lord continue to make His face shine on you and be gracious to you. May the Lord continue to look upon you with favor and give you peace as you join and lead this Faith@Home movement in your church. In the name of the Father, the Son and the Holy Spirit. Amen!

Ponder, Pray and Discuss

1. As a review, list the five dots that must be connected in order to have a successful launch of the Faith@Home movement in your church.

2. Which dots do you think will be easy for you to connect? Which dots do you think will take more time to connect?

3. Have the examples I've given and the testimonials of other people helped you to see that Faith@Home can make a difference in your church?

4. Has the fact that you'll have ongoing support helped you make a decision about whether or not to launch the Faith@Home movement in your church?

5. Have you decided to launch the Faith@Home movement in your church? Why or why not?

Associate Pastor
Ministry Profile

CHRIST COMMUNITY CHURCH

Nanaimo, British Columbia, Canada

Christ Community Church desires to be a vibrant spiritual community that shapes the next generation of God's Champions.

Terms:	Permanent, Full-time
Reports to:	Lead Pastor and Council
Purpose:	(1) To assist the leadership and congregation of Christ Community Church in encouraging and equipping the home to be the primary place where faith is lived, nurtured and shared. (2) To assist in implementing our vision, mission and core values. (3) To partner in building a vibrant spiritual community.

Preferred Education, Experience, Skills and Spiritual Maturity
- Spiritual and emotional maturity, with an intimate relationship with God through Jesus Christ, as evidenced by healthy prayer and devotions disciplines.
- Ordained within the CRC denomination or on track to becoming ordained.
- Leadership skills including collaborative, time management, organizational and administration skills; as well as an awareness of his or her own leadership style.

- Experience with volunteer management; including recruiting and coaching.
- Demonstrated interpersonal skills that include the following:

  - Positive and encouraging in attitude, with strong communication skills.
  - High personal integrity, with the ability to gain trust and respect.
  - Able to recognize and appreciate the giftedness and differences in people.
  - Able to mediate differences, using conflict resolution tools.

- Preferred experience in leading youth, children and/or family ministries.

Expectations
- Invest time, treasures and talents in Christ Community Church and its congregation; to commit long term to this church and to the community it serves.
- Champion the *Building Faith at Home* concepts; encouraging all generations to use their gifts in fulfilling our vision.
- Seek and accept coaching, outside training and on-the-job training where needed.

Duties and Responsibilities
- Recruit and coach volunteer ministry team leaders from our congregation who, through their ministries, will encourage and equip the home to be the primary place where faith is lived, nurtured and shared.
- Connect with these ministry team leaders on a regular basis to determine:

  - What Faith@Home focus they choose to celebrate.
  - What their next Faith@Home event might be.
  - What help and/or resources they need to facilitate that.

- How they can support other ministries' Faith@Home initiatives.

- Work with these ministry team leaders and the Board of Elders to coordinate Take It Home events on an annual basis.
- Attract new members by engaging and networking in the greater community of Nanaimo; creating an awareness of the resources and support we offer that encourage and equip the home.

Children, Youth and Family Ministry Pastor Job Description

by Dr. Dick Hardel

Youth and family ministry is a new paradigm that has a focus on faith formation.* Some congregations have begun to use new titles for this position of leadership. Some new titles are minister to the Christian home, director of faith formation, director of faith nurture in the home, and director of discipleship in the home. These new titles are used to move the members of the congregation away from the old paradigm of youth group or youth ministry separated from the whole ministry of the congregation.

From the study of research on faith formation, Vibrant Faith Ministries has shared that the home is the primary place to teach and nurture faith. The congregation is in partnership with the home and works to strengthen the adults in the home to pass on the faith. In this new paradigm, a director of youth and family ministry must work with the parents and other primary caregivers as well as the children and youth of the congregation and community. This ministry must be built from a new vision, rather than around the personality of a person.

At Vibrant Faith Ministries, when we talk about youth ministry, we mean from pre-birth to about age 35. It is about passing on the faith and nurturing the faith. When we talk about family, we do not mean one specific type of family. We mean working with every type of family to grow in Christ. This includes single adults. Their family may be made up of two or three very close friends who share faith, values and friendship. That also is family. Family goes beyond immediate blood relatives and includes mentors, friends and others outside the household.

Often, when a congregation seeks to fill a part-time position in youth and family ministry, it is because the congregation cannot financially afford a full-time position. However, the expectations of the leadership of the congregation often equal that of a full-time position.

Since the concept of youth and family is a new paradigm, it may be difficult for a congregation to find a person who is trained in this new model. My first suggestion is to search for someone who has the heart and the call for ministry. It may be someone from the congregation. Vibrant Faith Ministries, the Certification School at Wartburg Theological Seminary, and a few other organizations provide continuing education and critical skills courses in youth and family ministry. This is an option to consider and may be easier than trying to locate someone outside of your congregation with the passion and skills for this ministry.

Key Attributes of a Director of Youth and Family Ministry

1. Loves the Lord and can express his or her faith well
2. Loves the Church
3. Loves to be with children, youth and their families
4. Is a director and not just a doer
5. Understands ministry as team
6. Is willing to receive coaching, outside training and on-the-job training
7. Faith is founded in a theology of the cross (grace-oriented), and lives a faith-filled and faithful life in response to God's grace. (In other words, this person models the gospel of Jesus, the Christ.)

Everything else can be taught. But the attributes listed above are essential.

Other Essential Things
to Consider

- Understanding Youth and Family Ministry: Youth and family ministry is a holistic and intergenerational approach to ministry. It is primarily not about children, youth or families. It is primarily about Jesus. It is about discipleship and passing on the faith. It is not just children's ministry or youth ministry. It is everything that God is doing in the community through the congregation. Thus, a director of youth and family ministry must work with the whole ministry team of the congregation, have a clear understanding of the vision and mission of the congregation and understand faith formation.

- There are four imperatives in youth and family ministry:
  1. Faith-focused Christian education
  2. Strengthening family relationships
  3. Congregation as family
  4. Christian youth subculture

- There are four keys to nurturing faith in the home:
  1. Caring conversation (includes faith talk)
  2. Devotions in the home
  3. Family service (in the neighborhood and community)
  4. Rituals and traditions in the home

- The congregation must offer a salary so that the director can raise a family and stay for many years.

- The congregation should financially support the ongoing training of the director of youth and family ministry.

- The director of youth and family ministry must know how the congregation is structured and functions.

- The job description must clearly state that the director of youth and family ministry is to equip and mentor parents and other adults as well as youth with leadership skills to do the ministry. The job is to build on God's vision, equip families for their ministries, direct the ministries and support the doers of ministry.

• For the health and wellbeing of the director of youth and family ministry and the longevity of the ministry, the director of youth and family should develop strong, spiritual disciplines (i.e., personal prayer, devotional life, daily reading of Scripture, faithful and regular attendance at worship, and develop a prayer support team).

• The director of youth and family, as with all other members of the ministry team, is accountable to the vision of what God is doing in and through the congregation. All the ministries in youth and family ministry must connect to the vision of the congregation.

• The director of youth and family ministry should develop a discipling ministry of leadership for both youth and adults in the congregation and community.

• The congregation should develop a clear plan for future growth of the person and the position. It is helpful to find a coach for a person in a new position.

• The congregation's budget for youth and family ministry must reflect a good salary with benefits, support for the planning and carrying out of ministries, and continued education of staff and other lay volunteers to be trained.

---

* Article used with the kind permission of Dr. Dick Hardel, Vibrant Faith Ministries (formerly known as the Youth and Family Institute), located in Minneapolis, Minnesota. For more information, call them toll-free (1- 877-239-2492) or visit their website (http://vibrantfaith.org).

Holding a Faith@Home Leadership Summit

by Mark Holmen and Dave Teixeira

This outline for holding a Faith@Home Leadership Summit has been reprinted from *Take It Home: Inspiration and Events to Help Parents Spiritually Transform Their Children*.[1] Corresponding Power Point slides are available on the DVD provided with that implementation guide.

I. Opening: Create an Inviting Atmosphere
    A. Food, decorations, music playing, name tags, etc.
    B. Have people sit at round tables in their ministry teams. For example:
        1. Table 1—Music and worship leaders (lay and staff)
        2. Table 2—Adult ministry leaders (men's ministry, women's ministry, etc.)
        3. Table 3—Children's ministry leaders
        4. Table 4—Youth ministry leaders
        5. Table 5—Elders/general board
    C. Begin by thanking people for giving their most precious commodity—their time—to participate in this summit meeting.

II. Time of Worship (30 minutes)
    A. Take time to refuel your leaders through a time of praise and worship.

B. Pray for the Holy Spirit to come and give your team unity and vision for a family ministry that will transform the lives of families in your community.

C. Add your own worship slides.

III. Session I: What Are We Accomplishing? (60 minutes)

A. Opening discussion starter: Before we get started, an important point to note is that when you use the word "family," you are talking about every form of family. A single person in a nursing home is a form of family, a dual-income no-kids (DINK) couple is a form of family, etc.

1. Tell the audience that a *USA Today* article once stated that there were over 28 forms of family.

2. State that when you say the word "family," you will be talking about *all* 28 forms of family.

3. Share the following quote from Peter Benson, Director of Search Institute: "As the family goes so goes the future of the church. Religious life in the home is more influential than the church."

B. As a group, discuss the following questions:

1. How are families in our church and community going today?

2. If this is the future of the Church, what does that mean for our church?

3. Do you agree that religious life in the home is more influential than the Church? Why or why not?

C. In a national survey by Search Institute titled "The Most Significant Religious Influences," teenagers were asked to identify what factors influenced them to have faith. Their answers were quite revealing:

1. Influence #1—Mother

2. Influence #2—Father

3. Influence #3—Pastor

4. Influence #4—Grandparent

5. Influence #5—Sunday School

6. Influence #6—Youth Group

7. Influence #7—Church Camp

8. Influence #8—Retreats[2]

D. But the key finding was that Mom and Dad were two to three times more influential than any church program!

E. How is religious life in the home today? Have the participants guess the answers to the following Search Institute survey of more than 11,000 participants from 561 congregations across 6 different denominations. Remember, these are the responses from churched teenagers!

1. What percentage of teenagers have a regular dialogue with their mother on faith/life issues? (12 percent)

2. What percentage of teens have a regular dialog with their father on faith/life issues? (5 percent)

3. What percentage of teenagers have experienced regular reading of the Bible and devotions in the home? (9 percent)

4. What percentage of youth have experienced a service-oriented event with a parent as an action of faith? (12 percent)[3]

F. Share the following quote from George Barna: "We discovered that in a typical week, fewer than 10 percent of parents who regularly attend church with their kids read the Bible together, pray together (other than at meal times) or participate in an act of service as a family unit. Even fewer families—1 out of 20—have any type of worship experience together with their kids, other than while they are at church during the typical month."[4]

G. Discuss together the following questions:

1. Based on these statistical realities, how is religious life in the home today?

2. What do you think has caused this reality?

3. What has the church done or not done to cause or address this reality?

H. Let's hear what others are saying (share the following quotes):

1. "For all their specialized training, church professionals realize that if a child is not receiving basic

Christian nurture in the home, even the best teachers and curriculum will have minimal impact. Once-a-week exposure simply cannot compete with daily experience where personal formation is concerned."[5]

2. "When a church—intentionally or not—assumes a family's responsibilities in the arena of spiritually nurturing children, it fosters an unhealthy dependence upon the church to relieve the family of its biblical responsibility."[6]

3. "Most certainly father and mother are apostles, bishops, and priests to their children, for it is they who make them acquainted with the gospel."[7]

4. "Most teenagers and their parents may not realize it, but a lot of research in the sociology of religion suggest that the most important social influence in shaping young people's religious lives is the religious life modeled and taught to them by their parents."[8]

5. And finally, my favorite quote from Dr. Roland Martinson of Luther Seminary: "What we ought to do is let the kids drop their parents off at church, train the parents and send them back into their mission field, their home, to grow Christians!"

I. Let's look at one other source: the Bible!
    1. Have someone read the following passages:
       a. Deuteronomy 6:1-12
       b. Joshua 24:14-16
       c. Psalm 78
    2. Discuss how faith at home is a biblical mandate!

J. Review: What have we discovered?
    1. Religious life in the home is more influential than the Church.
    2. Mom and Dad are two to three times more influential than any church program.
    3. *Yet*, faith talk, devotions, Bible reading, prayer and service aren't happening in the home.
    4. Faith at home is biblically mandated and what God intended.

K. Conclusion: Therefore, we need to get religious life, Christ and Christlike living back into the center of every home!

  1. Close with the following quote from Mark Holmen: "I believe one of the greatest existing challenges facing the Christian Church today is trying to figure out how we can equip the home to once again be the primary place where faith is nurtured through our existing ministry structures."

  2. State that this will be the focus of our next session.

L. Take a 30-minute break.

IV. Session II: Becoming a Valuable Partner (minimum 2 hours)

A. Open with the following quote from George Barna: "The local church should be an intimate and valuable partner in the effort to raise the coming generation of Christ followers and church leaders, but it is the parents whom God will hold primarily accountable for the spiritual maturation of their children."[9]

B. Discuss the following together:

  1. Is your church currently a valuable partner in bringing Christ and Christlike living into the home?

  2. Do unchurched people recognize your church as a valuable partner for them as parents, or as a program center for their kids?

  3. Does your church have any of the following symptoms:

    a. An increasing number of parents who simply drop their children/youth off for the programs of the church but never attend themselves?

    b. A decreasing number of students attending or participating in the programs of the church as they get older?

    c. An increasing number of students and/or young adults who abandon their faith as they get older?

  4. If your church has any or all of these symptoms, you're not alone. These are the symptoms of a church that

has focused on having great programs and leaders who engage people at church but at the same time has gotten away from making the home—and Mom and Dad—the primary influencers of faith development.

5. Let's take a look at how we can equip the home to once again be the primary place where faith is nurtured through our existing ministry structures.

C. Go through the family ministry vision and Faith@Home-focused church model found in chapter 3.

1. Go through the add-a-silo versus the Faith@Home-focused church models [see pages 76-77].

2. Discuss what it means to become a Faith@Home-focused church versus a church with family ministry.

3. Tell the audience that you are now going to focus the rest of your time together on how to become a Faith@Home-focused church.

D. The five keys for becoming a Faith@Home-focused church:

1. Key #1—senior pastor buy in

a. Ask your senior pastor to share his/her passion and commitment for becoming a Faith@Home-focused church.

b. How has God put this vision on your pastor's heart?

c. How does your pastor see the Faith@Home focus fitting in to your overall church mission/vision/strategy?

2. Key #2—language matters

a. What are you going to call/name your Faith@Home focus? (Remember: the word "family" creates a barrier that prevents many people from buying into the idea.)

b. Does this language fit across all your ministries and within your mission/vision/strategy?

3. Key #3—a part of the strategy of the church

a. Does your church's mission/vision/strategy accurately reflect your commitment to be a Faith@Home-focused church?

    b. What changes could/should you make?

    c. How will these changes be shared by/with the congregation?

4. Key #4—confident humility

    a. How confident are you that Faith@Home is a God-ordained principle?

    b. Is Faith@Home something you are personally living?

    c. Are you willing to humbly launch and lead something that may take 5, 10, or even 15 years to see results?

5. Key #5—financial commitment

    a. What is the percentage of budgeted resources that your church spends on "church-based" ministries versus Faith@Home-focused efforts?

    b. What additional resources will be needed to fund your Faith@Home focus?

    c. How will those funds be secured?

6. Key #6—get all ministries involved

    a. Begin by sharing how each ministry of the church has a role to play in becoming a Faith@Home-focused church.

    b. Go through and explain the Take It Home events [see page 84] and how these can serve as the backbone for your Faith@Home initiative as a congregation.

    c. Give each ministry 30 to 60 minutes to discuss what they could do to help make the Faith@Home movement happen in their ministry area. Questions they should discuss include:

        i. How can we contribute to becoming a Faith@Home-focused church?

        ii. How can we partner with our people to bring Christ and Christlike living back into the home?

        iii. What Take It Home event(s) could we initiate or help make happen?

        iv. Is there another ministry we should partner with to help make this happen?

    d. Bring everyone back together and list the ideas each ministry came up with on a whiteboard.

    e. Organize the ideas by establishing the dates and times for each Take It Home event.

    f. Determine who will provide the leadership for each event.

7. Key #7—identify and empower a Faith@Home champion

    a. Who is someone in your church leadership who "bleeds" Faith@Home?

    b. What needs to happen so that that person can be empowered to champion Faith@Home across *all* the ministries?

    c. What needs to happen so that that person can continue to be empowered and resourced with some of the best Faith@Home ideas that are happening?

    d. Has he/she signed up for Faith@Home coaching?

    e. Can he/she attend one Faith@Home-focused conference per year?

    f. Does he/she have the funds to purchase Faith@Home-focused resources?

8. Key #8—preach Faith@Home

    a. How is your Faith@Home focus going to be represented during your weekend services?

    b. Will you have regular Faith@Home sermons and/or sermon series throughout the year?

    c. Will you have Take It Homework every Sunday?

    d. Will you incorporate intergenerational worship on holiday weekends?

9. Key #9—long-term commitment

    a. How long do you think it will take to reestablish the home as the primary place where faith is lived, expressed and nurtured?

b. How are you going to measure your Faith@Home progress?
c. What safeguards do you need to implement so that you won't lose your Faith@Home focus?

Frequently Asked Questions

As I travel across the country and even around the world sharing the Faith@Home movement with pastors and church leaders, these are some of the commonly asked questions I receive.

Q. Is this just an issue in the American Church?

A. Absolutely not. I recently spoke to a group of international church leaders from 13 different countries. When I finished, the response and desire from these leaders to have the Faith@Home movement brought to their countries was overwhelming! I've learned that the program-driven model is clearly established in Christian churches around the world, which also means there is a need for faith at home to exist all over the world. I wonder if this is one of the reasons why house churches are becoming increasingly popular and effective. House churches are naturally all about faith at home! Maybe we should learn from them.

Q. What if people resist or outright reject the idea of faith at home because they simply want an experience they can come to or a place where they can drop off their children?

A. I've never liked this question, because it forces us to do something we don't like to do: choose. Let me tell you what Joshua had to say about choosing: "If serving the LORD seems undesirable to you, then choose for yourselves this day whom you will serve, whether the gods your forefathers served beyond the River, or the gods of the Amorites, in whose land you are living. But as for me and my household, we will serve the LORD" (Josh. 24:15).

I've found that the majority of people will embrace a Faith@Home movement, especially when they experience Take It Home events for the first time and realize how serious a church has become about helping them as people and families to establish Christlike living in the home. Most people want to be healthier and stronger spiritually. So when a church provides ways to help them be healthier and stronger, they're both surprised and elated.

Still, some people will always simply want the "professionals" to do it for them. They don't want the church to ask them to do anything more or to change anything about them or their way of life. They just want to drop off their kids so that the church can teach the faith and instill good values in their children while Mom and Dad head to the health club or supermarket.

At Ventura Missionary Church, when we were confronted with this situation, we simply told people that we might not be the right church for them. When I met with visitors and every new-member class, I clearly let people know that if they were looking for a church where they could drop off their children and expect us to teach them the faith, we were not the right church for them.

As pastors and church leaders, we have to make a choice. Is faith at home important or not? For me, I decided that this was a nonnegotiable matter. So we let our people know that. And then, by the way we structured our ministries, we showed them that faith at home is a nonnegotiable matter.

Q. What if the parents don't show up for the Take It Home events?

A. I would like to say that we had 98 percent turnout from the first day we offered a Take It Home event, but that wouldn't be accurate. Over a few years, we've grown to the place where we have this kind of turnout by offering the Take It Home events through our normal Sunday School or youth ministry programs and by making sure the events are valuable and equipping. Still, we do have a few children who show up without parents. So what do we do with them?

First, we ask them where their parents are. Many times, the parents simply forgot about the event and went to the worship service.

If that's the case, we actually go and get the parents out of the service. In fact, I've even made the announcement, "If you're the parent of a second-grader who is enrolled in our Sunday School, you need to go and join your child at his or her Take It Home event that is taking place now in room . . ."

If we can't locate the child's parents, we then ask the Sunday School teacher of that class to serve as a surrogate parent for that event. This teacher encourages the students to do the faith skill with their parents when they get home, and the teacher also calls the parents after the event to explain the faith skill that the children learned to do with their parents at home. In most cases, these parents are the first to show up at the next Take It Home event the following year!

Q. How do you incorporate new families who join the church and have missed previous Take It Home events?

A. In most cases, the family can simply start where they are and move forward. For example, if a new family comes to our church with a teenage daughter, we won't start by trying to teach the parents how to start blessing her each evening. Her first Take It Home event might be the "Dating, Kissing, Sex and Stuff" retreat, where we help the parents and teen to have a shared experience and discussion about these critically important issues.

Would it have been beneficial for this family to have experienced the previous Take It Home events and to have learned how to pray together, read the Bible together, and so forth? Absolutely. Yet each Take It Home event is a targeted, age-specific event that doesn't require participation in previous events. In many cases, a family will ask us if they can have some of the resources or ideas we shared in previous Take It Home events. We gladly make those resources available.

Q. Will the older generation support this movement?

A. In a word, yes. The bigger question is, will the church include them in the movement? Senior adults need to be included in faith at home because of the vital role they can play. One idea for incorporating seniors into a Faith@Home movement is to hold a Meddling Grandparenting workshop. In this event, the church intentionally equips the senior adults to be faith mentors in the lives of their grandchildren. Another idea is to start a faith-mentoring program to build relationships between the senior adults and the students. In addition, the church can include senior adults in Take It Home events for testimonies or as church grandparents who simply participate with the families.

Q. How do you incorporate or take single people into consideration?

A. Singles need faith at home as much as married people. For example, I've been asked to bless the apartments of single adults in my congregation, which becomes a powerful testimony that they're going to make sure Christlike living happens in their home. This is an amazing commitment for a 22-year-old to make when a more natural temptation might be for him or her to have the apartment be a party place. It is important for the church to include singles in the discussion about faith at home and also to ask them how they can help make the single's ministry more Faith@Home driven. You'll find that many of them appreciate this change in focus.

In addition, the church should invite people in its singles ministry to engage in and even lead Take It Home events. At VMC, the singles ministry decided to put together a Halloween Monster Mash event for parents and children to attend as an alternative to trick-or-treating. The singles group provided all the leadership for the event. Families that attended were blessed as their children participated in a safe, faith-nurturing family event on Halloween.

Q. Who do you turn to for ideas and resources for your movement?

A. The first answer that comes to mind is *everywhere*. VMC's family ministry team and I were continually looking for ideas and resources that could be used at home. We searched Christian bookstores, catalogs, websites and anywhere else we could think of to find the most cost effective or free resources possible. Very seldom did we use the same resource for more than five years, because it always seemed like another resource would come out that was a little better and often a little less expensive.

I also turn to friends who are like-minded in the way they lead their churches. Tim, one of my best friends, was a youth and family pastor. We frequently called or emailed each other or got together just to share ideas. Proverbs 27:17 says, "Iron sharpens iron," and that's always been the case for me. Tim would take a resource, program or idea and put his Faith@Home twist on it, and before long, I would be applying it in my church. This was the reason we created a Faith@Home website (www.faithathome.com)—so that like-minded people could share ideas and resources with one another.

Q. What would you say to pastors in training?

A. First, I would point out that they probably won't receive any Faith@Home training in Bible college or seminary. So faith at home is a perspective they will need to bring to their training classes or seminars.

This is both a challenge and an opportunity. It's a challenge because their professors won't be prepared for them questioning what they're learning with this perspective. This might create some "we haven't done it that way before" tension. Higher education isn't known for quickly embracing new ways of looking at things. In my own experience, I've found myself running into a brick wall as I try to challenge educators to think beyond the church to the home. They've been looking at things through church lenses so long that it's difficult for them to see things any other way.

However, for pastors in training, this presents a great opportunity to don a set of Faith@Home lenses as they go through training. They can get a jump start from the very beginning of their calling and career. I wish I'd had my perspective change when I went through seminary. I would have looked at things differently. I only saw things through a lens of how to teach or apply this at church.

ENDNOTES

Chapter 1: What Are We Accomplishing?

1. George Barna, *Transforming Children into Spiritual Champions* (Ventura, CA: Regal, 2003), p. 81.
2. ECE study, Search Institute, Minneapolis, Minnesota.
3. Barna, *Transforming Children into Spiritual Champions*, p. 78.
4. George Barna, *Revolution* (Carol Stream, IL: Tyndale House Publishers, 2005), pp. 48-49.
5. George Barna, www.barna.org/barna-update/article/16-teensnext-gen/147-most-twentysomethings-put-christianity-on-the-shelf-following-spiritually-active-teen-years.
6. T. C. Pinkney, "Report to the Southern Baptist Convention Executive Committee," Nashville, Tennessee, September 18, 2001. Pinkney, vice-president of the Southern Baptist Convention, reports that 70 percent of teenagers involved in church youth groups stop attending church within two years of their high school graduation. In another study from the Southern Baptist Council on Family Life, they found 88 percent of the children raised in evangelical homes leave church at the age of 18, never to return. See "Southern Baptist Council on Family Life report to Annual Meeting of the Southern Baptist Convention," 2002. http://www.sbcannualmeeting.net/sbc02/newsroom/newspage.asp?ID=261.
7. Reggie McNeal, citing youth ministry specialist Dawson MacAlister, *The Present Future* (San Francisco, CA: Jossey-Bass, 2003), p. 4.
8. David Kinnaman, *UnChristian* (Grand Rapids, MI: Zondervan Publishing, 2008), p. 42. Used by permission.
9. Chart on Faith Influence in Youth reprinted with permission from *Effective Christian Education: A National Study of Protestant Congregations*, © 1990 Search Institute SM. No other use is permitted without prior permission from Search Institute, 615 First Avenue NE, Minneapolis, MN 55413; www.search-institute.org.
10. Search Institute is a nonprofit, nonsectarian research and educational organization that advances the wellbeing and positive development of children and youth through applied research, evaluation, consultation, training, and the development of publications and practical resources for educators, youth-serving professionals, parents, community leaders, and policy makers (www.search-institute.org).
11. Christian Smith with Melinda Lundquist Denton, *Soul Searching* (New York: Oxford Press, 2005), p. 56.
12. Marjorie Thompson, *The Family as Forming Center* (Nashville, TN: Upper Room Books, 1996), p. 26.
13. Barna, *Transforming Children into Spiritual Champions*, p. 81.
14. Peter L. Benson, *All Kids Are Our Kids* (San Francisco, CA: Jossey-Bass, 2006), p. 107.
15. Dawson McAlister, *Finding Hope for Your Home* (Irving, TX: Shepherd Ministries, 1996), n.p.
16. Barna, *Transforming Children into Spiritual Champions*, p. 24.
17. Martin Luther, "The Estate of Marriage, 1522" in Walther Brand, ed., *Luther's Works* (Philadelphia: Fortress Press, 1962), p. 46.
18. Jack Eggar, cited in Larry Fowler, *Rock-Solid Kids* ((Ventura, CA: Gospel Light, 2004), p. 7.

Chapter 2: Do We Care?

1. Mark DeVries, *Family-Based Youth Ministry* (Downers Grove, IL: InterVarsity Press, 1994), back cover.

2. George Barna, *Revolution* (Carol Stream, IL: Tyndale House Publishers, 2005), p. 35.

3. DeVries, *Family-Based Youth Ministry,* back cover.

Chapter 3: What Should We Do About It?

1. Marjorie Thompson, *The Family as Forming Center* (Nashville, TN: Upper Room Books, 1996), p. 144.

2. George Barna, *Revolution* (Carol Stream, IL: Tyndale House Publishers, 2005), p. 35.

3. Ibid.

4. Larry Fowler, *Rock-Solid Kids* (Ventura, CA: Gospel Light, 2004), p. 25.

5. Thompson, *The Family as Forming Center,* p. 23.

6. Christian Smith with Melinda Lundquist Denton, *Soul Searching: The Religious and Spiritual Lives of American Teenagers* (New York: Oxford University Press, 2005), p. 57.

7. Jonathan Edwards, quoted in Clyde A. Holbrook, *The Ethics of Jonathan Edwards: Morality and Aesthetics* (Ann Arbor, MI: University of Michigan Press, 1973), p. 83.

8. Barna, *Revolution,* p. 24.

9. This idea comes from Vibrant Faith Ministries (formerly known as the Youth and Family Institute) located in Minneapolis, Minnesota. More information is available at their website: www.youthandfamilyinstitute.org.

10. *Take It Home: Inspiration and Events to Help Parents Spiritually Transform Their Children* is published by Gospel Light, located in Ventura, California. Contact them at 1-800-446-7735, or visit their website www.gospellight.com.

11. The Superman Prayer usually consists of the following words sung to the *Superman* movie theme:

> *Thank You, God, for giving us food.*
> *Thank You, God, for giving us food.*
> *For the food that we eat.*
> *For the friends that we meet.*
> *Thank You, God, for giving us food. Amen.*

Or this variation:

> *Thank You, Lord, for giving us food.*
> *Thank You, Lord, for giving us food.*
> *And for our daily bread,*
> *For we like to be fed.*
> *Thank You, Lord, for giving us food.*

Chapter 4: What Are the Keys to Becoming a Faith@Home-focused Church?

1. George Barna, *Revolution* (Carol Stream, IL: Tyndale House Publishers, 2005), pp. 25-26.

2. I heard Bill Hybels deliver this talk, titled "Four Things You Must Do," at a Leadership Summit. The talk has been redistributed and is available through the Willow Creek Association's Defining Moments series. To order a copy, contact the Willow Creek Customer Service Center at 1-800-570-9812, or visit the website at www.willowcreek.com.

3. Thom Rainer, *Breakout Churches: Discover How to Make the Leap* (Grand Rapids, MI: Zondervan, 2005), p. 58.

4. Ibid., pp. 57-58.

Chapter 5: What Are the Traps to Avoid, and What Would We Win?

1. Robert Greenleaf, *Servant Leadership: A Journey into the Nature of Legitimate Power and Greatness* (Mahwah, NJ: Paulist Press, 1977), p. 29.

2. Rolf Garborg, *The Family Blessing: Creating a Spiritual Covering for Your Family's Future* (Lakeland, FL: White Stone Books, 2003). For more information, visit Rolf's website: www.rolfgarborg.com.

3. For a list of these developmental assets, see the Search Institute website at www.search-institute.org.

4. Copyright © 1997 by Search Institute, Minneapolis, MN. Used by permission. All rights reserved.

5. Ibid. Data on "Succeeds in School" and "Volunteer Service" based on the original framework of thirty assets. Peter L. Benson, *All Kids Are Our Kids* (San Francisco: Jossey-Bass, 1997), p. 60. Used by permission.

6. Glenn A. Seefeldt and Eugene C. Roehlkepartain, *Tapping the Potential: Discovering Congregation's Role in Building Assets in Youth.* ©1995 by Search Institute, Minneapolis, MN. Used by permission.

7. Dave Teixeira, *Take It Home: Inspiration and Events to Help Parents Spiritually Transform Their Children* (Ventura, CA: Gospel Light, 2008), p. 38.

Chapter 6: How Do We Connect the Dots and Keep Going?

1. John Maxwell, *The 21 Irrefutable Laws of Leadership: Follow Them and People Will Follow You* (Nashville, TN: Thomas Nelson, 1998), p. 225.

2. Mark Holmen and Dave Teixeira, *Take It Home: Inspiration and Events to Help Parents Spiritually Transform Their Children* (Ventura, CA; Regal Books, 2007); Mark Holmen, *Faith Begins at Home* (Ventura, CA: Regal Books, 2006).

3. Holmen and Teixeira, *Take It Home*, p. 35.

Appendix 3: Holding a Faith@Home Leadership Summit

1. Mark Holmen and Dave Teixeira, *Take It Home: Inspiration and Events to Help Parents Spiritually Transform Their Children* (Ventura, CA: Regal Books, 2007), pp. 43-48.

2. For the complete results, see Mark Holmen, *Faith Begins at Home* (Ventura, CA: Regal Books, 2006), p. 43.

3. *Effective Christian Education: A National Study of Protestant Congregations,* copyright 1990 by Search Institute SM. No other use is permitted without prior permission from Search Institute, 615 First Avenue NE, Minneapolis, MN 55413; www.search-institute.org.

4. George Barna, *Transforming Children into Spiritual Champions* (Ventura, CA: Regal Books, 2003), p. 78.

5. Marjorie Thompson, *Family, the Forming Center* (Nashville, TN: Upper Room Books, 1996).

6. Barna, *Transforming Children into Spiritual Champions*, p. 81.

7. Martin Luther, "The Estate of Marriage, 1522," quoted in Walther Brand, ed., *Luther's Works* (Philadelphia, PA: Fortress Press, 1962), p. 46.

8. Christian Smith and Melinda Lundquist Denton, *Soul Searching: A Vision of the Role of Family in Spiritual Formation* (New York: Oxford University Press, 2005), p. 56.

9. Barna, *Transforming Children into Spiritual Champions*, p. 83.

MARK HOLMEN

has worked with families for more than 20 years, serving as a youth and family pastor in three congregations. He has been a national consultant, speaker, trainer and author for the Youth and Family Institute. From 2002 to 2009, Mark was the senior pastor of Ventura Missionary Church in Ventura, California, where, in addition to serving his own congregation, he also helped other congregations equip the home to be the primary place where faith is nurtured. In 2009, after seven years as the senior pastor of Ventura Missionary Church, Mark turned his full-time focus to the growing Faith@Home movement, which is supported by the Willow Creek Association and Focus on the Family. Mark is the author of *Faith Begins at Home, Faith Begins @ Home Devotions, Faith Begins @ Home Prayer, Faith Begins @ Home Dad,* and is co-author of *Faith Begins @ Home Mom* (with his wife, Maria) and *Take It Home* (with Dave Teixeira). For more information, please contact Mark at:

WWW.FAITHATHOME.COM

More Resources by Mark Holmen

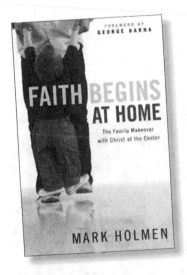

Also Available from Mark Holmen

Faith Begins @ Home Devotions
ISBN 978.08307.52294
ISBN 08307.52293

Faith Begins @ Home Prayer
ISBN 978.08307.52119
ISBN 08307.52110

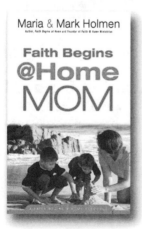

Faith Begins @ Home Mom
ISBN 978.08307.52317
ISBN 08307.52315

Faith Begins @ Home Dad
ISBN 978.08307.52300
ISBN 08307.52307